BOOST
YOUR
INTERVIEW
IQ

Revised and Expanded
Second Edition

Carole Martin

New York   Chicago   San Francisco   Lisbon   London   Madrid   Mexico City
Milan   New Delhi   San Juan   Seoul   Singapore   Sydney   Toronto

The *McGraw·Hill* Companies

1 2 3 4 5 6 7 8 9 10   DOC/DOC   1 8 7 6 5 4 3 2

ISBN   978-0-07-179746-7
MHID 0-07-179746-7

e-ISBN   978-0-07-179747-4
e-MHID 0-07-179747-5

McGraw-Hill books are available at special quantity discounts to use as premiums and sales promotions or for use in corporate training programs. To contact a representative, please e-mail us at bulksales@mcgraw-hill.com.

This book is printed on acid-free paper.

To the thousands of clients I've coached over the years,
thank you.
You have been my teachers
while I have been your coach.

To all the thousands of people who are seeking jobs—
who have gone to interview after interview
without receiving an offer—may this book give you
the confidence and answers you need
to get offers in the future.

To my wonderful family—all of you—who have
always been there for me, no matter what.

Contents

PART I
The Interview IQ Test:
Test Your Interview IQ—Questions and Answers

PART II
The Surefire Way to Boost Your Score

PART III
Management and Executives

PART IV
Career Changers and Reentry

PART V
Students and New Graduates

Foreword

I was excited to hear that Carole Martin was updating and expanding her classic book, *Boost Your Interview IQ*. Since 2004, I have recommended this book to hundreds of job seekers and have consistently heard positive feedback after their interviews. If you are in a job search, you need this book—or you could be competing with others who have already mastered Carole's interview strategies.

Wouldn't it be great to get an interview cheat sheet that includes the questions you will be asked along with the best possible answers? Of course that's not going to happen, but this book does the next best thing—arming you with proven strategies and techniques to handle just about any challenging question or scenario.

There are other helpful interviewing books on the market, but Carole's approach is unique. Not only does she include sample interview questions along with possible answers, but she analyzes each response and explains the rationale for the strongest answers. You will be able to determine your "interview IQ" through her innovative Interview IQ Test and see why some answers to interview questions work while others do not. You will learn to recognize different interview techniques so that you can better structure your responses. You will also learn what occurs on the other side of the hiring desk, giving you a better understanding of what employers are looking for when interviewing candidates.

In this updated edition, Carole expands the practice sections that are applicable to any career and adds new sections specifically for students, new graduates, managers, career changers, and people reentering the workforce. You will learn what "Key Factors" are and how to identify them, and how to use online resources as tools to help you improve your interview performance.

For most people, going on job interviews ranks right up there with dental visits and tax preparation—not exactly fun, but necessary. You can ease the pain by making sure you are prepared. Whether you're new to interviewing or are a seasoned pro, you'll find great advice and adaptable techniques that will improve your confidence, help you "sell" yourself during interviews, and produce more job offers.

Carole's expertise as an interview coach is unsurpassed. Her dynamic style has helped thousands of people improve their interview results and outperform their peers. She also trains and manages a certification program for other interview coaches. When I met Carole and attended one of her interview tips workshops, I was struck not only by her contagious enthusiasm and energy but also by her insightful ideas on how to excel at job interviews.

As you read this book, think of Carole as your personal interview advisor—your guide on how to "boost your interview IQ" and ace even the most challenging job interview.

—Kim Isaacs,
Director of ResumePower.com, Monster's Resume Expert,
and coauthor of *The Career Change Resume*
Doylestown, PA

Introduction

I n 2004, McGraw-Hill published my first book on the subject of interviewing—*Boost Your Interview IQ*. It has been very well received and has sold well in the United States and other countries. A great deal has happened in the world since that publication, both in the world of work and in our way of communicating. There are new ways to reach out and connect with people, and in turn for people to check you out. The world has become a smaller playing field. But at the same time, the opportunities have become more diverse.

It is now time to update this guidebook with stronger examples so that you can compete in a tougher, leaner job market. I am very excited to present a new, improved edition of *Boost Your Interview IQ*.

So what's new?

The readers' favorite part of the book—the Interview IQ Test with 50 questions and 150 possible answers—has been updated, improved, and expanded. And in addition to the 50 questions, we've added 30 questions with 90 possible answers. The additional questions are included in three new sections:

Management and Executives (Part 3)

Career Changers and Reentry (Part 4)

Students and New Graduates (Part 5)

These sections will focus on answers for the specific groups who may be asked questions pertinent to their experience, area of expertise, or situation. This does not mean that these questions cannot be used by everyone. Anyone can use them to determine what makes one answer stronger than another.

There are new examples of answers to the basic general interview questions as well as to the behavioral questions. More and more employers are using behavioral questions in interviews to determine if applicants are merely saying that they can do something or whether they can prove that they can do something through an example of past behavior.

Behavioral questions require an answer that offers an example, or "a story," of a time when you did something. A behavioral question will sound something like "Tell me about a time when . . ." or "Describe a situation when . . ." The secret to answering a behavioral question is in the way you tell the story, in as succinct a manner as possible. One of the techniques that you will learn in this book is how to use a simple formula—a storytelling technique—that will make your stories interesting and at the same time make your point. Once you learn this skill, you will be able to give excellent answers to behavioral questions every time.

You will also find new material that will help you identify "key factors." This is, in my opinion, an extremely helpful tool because it allows you to take the employer's "wish list" and determine what the employer is looking for in a candidate. This tool will give you the clues you need to prepare your answers and stories ahead of time and in turn will help you feel more prepared and confident going into the interview.

The new sections add value to the various groups who are struggling in a tough job market.

Part 3, "Management and Executives," addresses difficult questions that may be asked in an interview. For some managers and executives, this will be the first interview in many years. If this is your situation, be assured that a quick brush-up course will put you back in the game quickly. By going back to the basics, you will be able to showcase your extensive background and stories in a focused and succinct manner.

Part 4, "Career Changers and Reentry," targets those who find themselves in the position of being a new player on a new field. If you have changed careers or are reentering the job market, it is likely that you may not have interviewed in a long time and may feel rusty or lost about where to begin. By focusing on those skills that are more "transferable" and emphasizing your personal traits, you will learn to demonstrate your ability in many diverse situations while still allowing the interviewer to see that you have experiences, in both life and work.

Part 5, "Students and New Graduates," offers help to people with little work experience to draw from. Part 5 provides examples of classroom and group activities, volunteer and club activities, and even some social situations. It demonstrates how you can use your life experience to show your strong qualities and illustrate how those qualities fit the desired factors.

In summary, what you're getting in this "new, improved, updated" book are tools and techniques to instill confidence in anyone who takes the time to prepare and practice for the interview. The goal of this new edition of *Boost Your Interview IQ* is to model answers so that you will be able to form your own responses to deliver examples that will impress and win over even the toughest interviewers.

A Breakthrough System for Showing That You Are the Best Person for the Job

This book is your passport to acing any interview. You'll learn to tell any interviewer not only that you can do the job but that you are the best person for the job. After working with the techniques presented throughout this book, you will be able to tell any interviewer confidently how you will bring your experiences from the past with you to the job and how you are the candidate that company wants to hire. It's a tough job market out there, and being able to show the interviewer that you are the best person for the job is essential. Otherwise, you will lose out to the competition, and another person will get the job.

By learning these interviewing techniques, you will obtain the tools that will prepare you to answer interview questions that have stumped you in the past. Some of the most difficult questions to answer are those that ask for specific examples. Whenever interviewers ask for examples or ask questions that begin with "Tell me about a time when," they are seeking a specific example to see how you work—in other words, your method of operation. The formal name for this method of questioning is *behavioral interviewing*. The people interviewing you are trying to learn how you performed in the past. The interviewers will use the examples you give in your answers to ascertain whether you have what it takes to do the job for the company. As the interviewers listen to your examples and stories, they begin to notice patterns in your behavior that help them determine whether you have the experience you claim to have on your résumé.

Selling Yourself as a Product

Myth. The best candidate always gets the job.

Reality. The candidate who sells himself or herself most effectively always gets the job!

Interviewing is about selling. In a job interview, you sell yourself as a solution to the hiring manager's problem. It's a straightforward process:

An employer has a problem: work to be done. The first step the employer takes is to define what qualifications are necessary—a wish list—for the type of person who best fits the position. A posting is entered on the Internet or an ad is placed in the newspaper with the hope of finding the "best" person for the job. In a normal job market, an employer will settle for a match of 80 percent of the requirements; when the job market is tight, the employer has such a vast pool of candidates to choose from that the percentage rises to 100 percent and then some. In these kinds of market conditions, people giving interviews frequently ask, "What else do you have to offer in addition to the basics required?"

You, as the job seeker, see the ad or posting and know that you are the perfect person for the job. You have most or all of the qualifications and know that you can do the job. You submit your résumé and wait for the phone call to be invited for an interview so that you can convince the employer that you are the solution to the problem and the best person for the job.

When you receive the call inviting you to an interview, you are delighted. It would be nice if the excitement lasted and you sailed through the interview process and got a job offer every time. However, life is not that simple, and neither is the interviewing process.

Often your initial excitement turns to fear and then to panic. "What if I don't have all the answers to the questions?" you ask yourself. "They probably will choose another candidate because things never work out for me," you tell yourself. "If only I didn't have to go through the interview process; I know I can do that job," you say to yourself.

All these feelings of questioning and self-doubt are normal. In fact, they are extremely normal. Most people hate interviewing. It's a judgment process, and who wants to go through that and face the possibility of a rejection?

By using the tools in this book and learning the specific interview storytelling techniques, you will begin to feel more in control and confident about going to your next interview. Instead of feeling that you are bragging about yourself, you will be focusing on what you have to offer and letting the interviewer know that you not only are qualified but are the best person for the job! This book will guide you in preparing your own stories and examples. Being prepared with your success stories will make a tremendous difference in the way you feel about interviewing.

By taking the Interview IQ Test and rating your ability to judge the strongest answers, you will see how good you are at judging what the interviewer will be interested in hearing. You then can write your own stories as a way to tell interviewers about your own experiences and back up your claims and statements.

Once you understand how to give an example of past behavior with an interesting story, you will be able to prove to the interviewer that you have the relevant experience that company wants in the person it will hire. When you have written stories that are specific and focused, you will feel more prepared and confident. That means more successful interviews—and more job offers.

Although the emphasis of this book is on the candidate, the information is appropriate for anyone desiring an in-depth, experiential approach to the interviewing process.

Feeling prepared = improved confidence = successful interview = job offer

How to Improve Your Interviewing Skills, Particularly with Behavioral Questions

More and more interviewers are using the technique of behavioral interviewing. In fact, according to the website for the Career Services center at the SUNY College at Brockport, more than 30 percent of companies now use behavioral interviewing as their preferred way to choose top candidates.

What this means is that interviewers interpret what you say about yourself and your past behavior as an indicator of how you will behave in the future. In other words, if you did it before, you can do it again. And so it is in your best interest to be able to demonstrate through the use of recent, relevant examples that you have done similar jobs with proven success. When the interviewer begins to see patterns and hear about successes on your past jobs, you will be considered a serious candidate for the job.

What differentiates behavioral questions from traditional interview questions is the way the question is asked.

Traditional Question

"What would you do if you had to deal with an angry customer?"

A traditional interview question gives you the chance to spin a fairy tale. You can use your imagination and tell a wonderful tale to answer this type of question.

It is quite different when the interviewer asks a behavioral question.

Behavioral Question

"You say you have 'great customer service skills.' Can you give me an example of a time when you had to deal with an angry customer?"

You now have the challenge of thinking about your past experiences and coming up with a specific example of a time when you dealt with an angry customer. If you have been in a customer service position, you may have too many stories to deal with. This is when preparation makes the difference and pays off. In Part 2 you will learn to read through a job posting description and pick out the key factors that will help you prepare your stories ahead of time, selecting those that make you look like the best person for the job.

The key to answering behavioral questions successfully is to be as specific as possible, particularly in relation to the position you are seeking.

The following test question is meant to serve as a warm-up exercise to get you ready to take the Interview IQ Test. A behavioral question is asked, and three possible answers are given: **[A]**, **[B]**, and **[C]**. It is your task to pick the answer you think is the *strongest* one. Put yourself in the role of the interviewer and try to determine which answer would impress you the most.

Exercise: A Sample Test Question

INTERVIEWER'S QUESTION

"Tell me about a time when you had to deal with an angry customer."

Select the strongest answer.

[A] A woman called and was yelling about a product that didn't work. I listened and let her vent. I then made sure that I understood all the facts and told her that I would call her back within the next two hours. I did some research and found that her product was still under warranty and that we could send her a replacement product at no charge. I called her back, and she was glad to hear that. She thanked me and asked for my supervisor's name so that she could report my efficient service.

[B] Since I work in customer service, this happens every day. Someone calls and yells at me, and I have to take it. Sometimes I can help the customer by making a suggestion or referring the customer somewhere else, but not always. I just try to stay calm and not get irritated. I know that the customers aren't yelling at me and that they are really frustrated. I try to help as much as I can.

[C] Every time I get one of these angry people, I have to just sit and listen. Some days it is difficult to hear all the complaints, but that's the nature of the job. I just try to not take it personally and to get through the day.

ANSWERS

The Strongest Answer

[A] This answer is the strongest one because it provides a specific example of your experience dealing with an angry customer. Through your example, the interviewer can recognize skills that are relevant to the job: the ability to communicate, listening skills, good customer service skills, patience, the ability to research facts, and good follow-through.

The Mediocre Answer

[B] This is not as strong an answer as **[A]** because it lacks an example. The interviewer may sense a good work ethic and attitude but doesn't hear an example of how you handled a stressful situation or learn about any experiences you have had in dealing with customers. This represents a missed opportunity.

The Weakest Answer

[C] This is the weakest answer because it has a negative tone; it is almost whiny. It does not demonstrate an attitude that is supportive of customer service and does not offer any examples of the skills you have used to deal with situations like this one. The interviewer does not learn how you deal with customers from this answer.

RATE YOURSELF

If you chose answer **[A]**, give yourself 5 points.

If you chose answer **[B]**, give yourself 3 points.

If you chose answer **[C]**, give yourself 0 points.

Do you get the idea of the story and why it is important? Interviewers listen for skills and behavior to see if you can do the job and if your résumé claims can be backed up. Interviewers will not always remember the answers, but they will remember the impressions the answers made. By giving a specific answer, one that directly answers the question asked, you will give an impression of someone who not only has the needed skills but also follows directions. In Part 2, you will learn techniques to make your stories as interesting and as focused as possible.

Bear in mind that this is not a test in the sense that you will pass or fail. It is an exercise to help you recognize the mistakes you might be making when answering questions and to help you prepare stronger answers in the future. It is a test to be taken over and over again, each time improving your sense of what makes a story stronger and boosting your Interview IQ. You can continue retaking the test until you get the score you desire.

Are you ready to try your hand at selecting the strongest answers by taking the Interview IQ Test? If so, it's time to move on to Part 1.

PART I

The Interview IQ Test

Test Your Interview IQ—
Questions and Answers

Take the Test and Rate Your Interviewing Ability

If you take the Interview IQ Test, you will have a measure of how you size up when answering some of the most frequently asked interview questions.

Whether you are new to interviewing or have had a lot of interviewing experience, the Interview IQ Test will give you a deeper understanding of what is involved in the questions from the interviewer's perspective. Even if you are "interview savvy," reading through the test will give you an updated perspective on current interviewing practices.

As in any book on interviewing, the answers provided should not be memorized and recited at an interview, resulting in canned- or robotic-sounding answers. You will have far more successful interviews if you answer the questions in a sincere and natural manner, giving the interviewer an opportunity to get to know you and hear how you work best. Use the answers as a guide in writing your own personal stories.

Canned answers are easy for an interviewer to spot because they sound like something anyone could say. For example:

> *Interviewer's Question.* "What are you looking for in your next job?"
>
> *Canned Answer.* "I want to work for a growth-oriented company where I can utilize my skills and learn and develop new skills."

Not using canned answers does not mean going into the interview and winging it. It means being prepared with your own answers that will make you feel confident and able to present what you have to offer in a succinct manner—with confidence.

IQ Test Instructions

After each Interviewer's Question, there are three possible answers to choose from: **[A]**, **[B]**, and **[C]**. It is your task to select the answer you think would be most effective in an interview situation. Choose the answer you think is the strongest. As you read through the choices, think the way the interviewer might think. Which answer provides an in-depth look at the candidate's skills and experiences?

When you've completed the test, check the answers that follow and assign yourself the points indicated next to your choice. The next step is to total your points and check your Interview Ability Rating.

Regardless of how you rate, take the test a second time and see if you can boost your Interview IQ score. By reading the examples several times, you will become comfortable with the types of questions you may encounter and get an idea of the strongest answers to those questions. Use the scorecard at the end of Part 1 every time you take the Interview IQ Test.

Tip Try rereading the Interview IQ Test the day before your next interview to refresh your memory on what makes an answer the strongest one.

When you feel satisfied that you have the hang of the technique and that your score is as high as you want it to be, you will be ready to start preparing your own stories. For instructions on creating your own answers, turn to Part 2 to learn the secrets of the trade and get an in-depth look at storytelling that will make it easier for you to write your own focused and concise stories.

The Test: Frequently Asked Interview Questions

The First 50 Questions

The following interview questions have been divided into general questions and behavioral questions. When you read through the questions and answers, you will get a sense of what differentiates a question as behavioral and what techniques are needed to answer this type of question. You will find that there are no right or wrong answers, but you will begin to see how some answers are stronger and more effective than others.

The Next 30 Questions

These questions have been divided into groups—Management and Executives (Part 3), Career Changers and Reentry (Part 4), and Students and New Graduates (Part 5). These questions are a combination of general and behavioral.

General Interview Questions

General questions are the questions most commonly used in interviews. There are no guarantees that these will be the specific questions asked in an interview, but if you are able to answer these basic questions, you will be able to answer most other questions with greater ease. These are "getting to know you" questions. This is where the interviewer gets to know your skills, strengths, weaknesses, motivators, and style. These questions also include information about what motivates you and when you have been satisfied in your work. In other words, they ask, "Who are you?" "What are you looking for?" and "How would you fit in here?"

Turn the page for the general section of the Interview IQ Test.

The Interview IQ Test: General Questions

INTERVIEWER'S QUESTION

[1] "Tell me about yourself."

Select the strongest answer

[A] I started my career as an associate accountant for a small firm after graduating from college. I then left that firm and was hired as an accountant for a larger firm, where I spent two years. After reaching a level where there was no further growth in that company, I left to take a job with a start-up company where I was the CFO. Unfortunately, financial issues started to occur in the past two years, and I was laid off.

[B] I am a high-energy person who is dependable and determined. I pride myself on my high work ethic and loyalty. Every performance appraisal I have ever received has commended me for my ability to stay focused under pressure. I am also a "people person" and know how to connect with people at all levels and build relationships. I am currently looking for a place where I will be able to grow and develop while contributing to a company's bottom line.

[C] I have experience working in the marketing and sales field for seven years. My area of expertise is my ability to use technology and social networking to reach desired customers. I was able to increase our customer base by 15 percent in my last job. My strength is my analytical ability combined with my people skills to build strong teams and networks. Anyone who has worked with me would tell you that I have a high work ethic and a great sense of humor that has gotten me through some tough times.

ANSWERS

The Strongest Answer

[C] This is the strongest answer because it actually gives an answer to the question. It addresses the question the interviewer is asking—tell me about "you." Although the interviewer wants to know about your background, he or she is attempting to know the person behind the résumé. This answer is a summary of who you are—your background, your expertise, your strength, and your skills.

The Mediocre Answer

[B] The problem with this answer is that it walks the interviewer through the résumé. The question was not "Walk me through your résumé." The question was "Tell me about yourself." These are two different questions. There is another problem with this answer even if the interviewer had asked to be walked through the résumé. The answer starts at the bottom of the résumé and moves up. When you answer the question starting back 3, 5, or even 10 years ago, it drags on; and by the time you have reached the information at the top of the résumé, the interviewer may have lost interest.

The Weakest Answer

[A] This answer is the least effective of the three because it offers very general information focusing primarily on traits rather than skills. Being a "people person" is a great trait, but the interviewer is looking for a combination of skills and traits. A good portion of this answer should be about skills and accomplishments so that the interviewer has a more comprehensive picture of who you are and what you can do or have done.

RATE YOURSELF

If you chose answer [C], give yourself 5 points.

If you chose answer [B], give yourself 3 points.

If you chose answer [A], give yourself 0 points.

INTERVIEWER'S QUESTION

[2] "Why did you leave (or why are you planning to leave) your last position?"

Select the strongest answer.

[A] As is happening in many companies today, there was a mass layoff at my last company. It would not have been my choice to leave the company, as I was doing work that I really liked and was told that my performance was above average. Because the company decided to take a different path and use more technology, many jobs were eliminated. I understand why the decision was made, and I am moving on to find satisfaction in a company where my skills can be utilized.

[B] I have been doing the same job for four years, and I am feeling that I will not have the chance to move up unless I move out. The work just isn't challenging anymore, and I need to have new challenges to be motivated. I am looking for a company where I can take on new challenges and grow. I need to grow and develop, and I see that opportunity at your company in this position. I am very excited about this opportunity.

[C] My last boss and I just did not see eye to eye. It's important to me that the company that I work for has the same values I have, and I decided that it would be a good time for me to look outside. I have set some career goals for myself and know that my current boss will not be supportive of me moving up within the company. What I am looking for is a job with a bigger company where I can contribute but also move on a career path that has more responsibility.

ANSWERS

The Strongest Answer

[**A**] This is the strongest answer not because it mentions the layoff but because it has an upbeat tone. You liked what you did and were hoping the layoff wouldn't happen. In other words, if it hadn't been for something out of your control, you would still be there. The answer indicates a good attitude toward an unfortunate incident. Carrying baggage such as being angry over a layoff is a big mistake. It is best to deal with your frustration before the interview and then let it go and move forward.

The Mediocre Answer

[**C**] This is a weaker answer than [**A**] because it sounds like you may be a person who has trouble getting along with others—specifically management. It's a good rule to not "bad-mouth" a manager or boss in an interview. It is natural to want to take on more responsibility, and it is also acceptable to quit a job; but this answer focuses on your boss and a values mismatch. Make sure you have answers about your values and what you want in a company and a boss.

The Weakest Answer

[**B**] This is the weakest answer because it sounds canned and focuses on your need to be challenged—and it uses the word *challenge* three times. An interviewer might be concerned that if you were that bored at your last job, you will find this job boring as well, or at least not "challenging." While companies look for people who want to grow and develop, that is not their goal in hiring. They want someone to solve the problem by filling this position.

RATE YOURSELF

If you chose answer [**A**], give yourself 5 points.

If you chose answer [**C**], give yourself 3 points.

If you chose answer [**B**], give yourself 0 points.

INTERVIEWER'S QUESTION

[3] "Why do you want to work here?"

Select the strongest answer.

[A] I have been selecting companies and organizations whose mission statements are in line with my personal values and business ethics, where I know I can use my past experiences to be excited about what this company offers its customers. I want to represent a company with a dynamic product portfolio, a company that is a market leader with the technologies and people in place to be successful. I want to perform, learn, and grow professionally, while being recognized for my contributions.

[B] I found the job posting on the Internet, and I have to admit that I hadn't heard of your company. But once I started doing my research, I was very impressed with what I saw and the direction in which your company is moving. As I went through the requirements of this job and matched them against my experience and skills, it just started to click into place. I believe I am a perfect match for this position. I have a great deal of experience doing this type of job, and your company values are in line with the values I am seeking in a job.

[C] When I saw this posting, I knew this was the job for me. I have always been a fan of your clothing line and buy at your stores all the time. I would really like to be able to say I work for this company. It's important to me that the company I work for have a good reputation and good products. I see this as a great opportunity for me to be with a top-notch company that I really feel good about.

ANSWERS

The Strongest Answer

[**B**] This is the strongest answer because it speaks to the question and lets the interviewer know how you came to be there—the journey. The answer reflects research on your part. When you compare and contrast what you have against what the company is looking for, you spell out the match. This answer reflects confidence that you believe in yourself and that you are the best candidate for the position. If you don't believe in yourself, why would anyone else believe in you? In an actual interview, you could spell out the relevant experience you have to show the interviewer the match in skills against requirements.

The Mediocre Answer

[**A**] This is a weaker answer than [**B**] because it is a typical canned answer. It is right out of a book and could be said by almost anyone. When you are in the interview, it is important that the interviewer get to know you as a person. Flattery will get you everywhere—but false flattery will get you nowhere. The interview is a conversation with another person, not a lecture. It is your job to converse in an engaging style by being "yourself."

The Weakest Answer

[**C**] This is the weakest answer. It emphasizes "you" and what you can get from the opportunity. While being a fan or customer of a company is good from the consumer point of view, the answer would be stronger if you looked at the business side of the situation, for instance, by talking about one of your favorite ads or marketing campaigns used by the company or by noting how the company is doing against its competitors. Tell the interviewer something that indicates how your role as a consumer relates to the job you are applying for. Simply being a fan or customer of a company does not get you any extra points in the interview process.

RATE YOURSELF

If you chose answer [**B**], give yourself 5 points.

If you chose answer [**A**], give yourself 3 points.

If you chose answer [**C**], give yourself 0 points.

INTERVIEWER'S QUESTION

[4] "What are your goals?"

Select the strongest answer.

[A] My immediate goal is to find a job in a growth-oriented company. My goal is to work for a company where I can grow and eventually become a marketing manager. I would like to manage a team of "handpicked" people to make an impact on the company's bottom line. I am interested in a company that is forward thinking.

[B] I want to work for a company that believes in cross-functional training. I think that is the best way to learn and see the bigger picture in a company. Eventually I hope to return to school to earn an MBA. I think that will broaden my knowledge so that one day I can own my own consultant company, working nationally or internationally.

[C] I like to break down goals into short-term goals, with the long term in mind. Right now I'm looking for a position in a company with a solid track record. I want to contribute to a team, bringing my extensive experience in this field to add to the team mix. Long-term goals will depend on the career path available at the company. Ideally, I would like to move progressively within a company.

ANSWERS

The Strongest Answer

[**C**] This is the strongest answer among the three choices. Since this an open-ended question, there is no right or wrong way to answer it. This answer is the best because it is open to opportunities that allow room for growth but doesn't lock you into goals that may not be realistic or are too rigid or specific.

The Mediocre Answer

[**B**] This answer starts out well and then takes a nosedive. While it pays to be honest, this answer could turn the interviewer off. The employer is looking for someone who will stick around and contribute to the company. It is not the company's goal to hire someone and train that person to become a competitor one day.

The Weakest Answer

[**A**] The problem with this answer is that it is too specific and could be a turn-down factor if the company does not have a career path that would allow an employee to reach this goal. It is best to stay away from answers that are narrow or inflexible.

RATE YOURSELF

If you chose answer [**C**], give yourself 5 points.

If you chose answer [**B**], give yourself 3 points.

If you chose answer [**A**], give yourself 0 points.

INTERVIEWER'S QUESTION

[5] "What are your strengths?"

Select the strongest answer.

[A] My strength is my strong people skills. I love working with people and helping them solve problems. My customers are very important to me, and I let them know it. In fact, some of my customers ask for me specifically when they call in. I consider some of them to be my friends. I love getting positive feedback from customers who tell me what a good job I am doing.

[B] My strengths are a combination of my technical skills and my ability to work with a variety of customers. I consider myself a data-mining expert, but what makes me stand out from the competition is my ability to work directly with customers and get to the root of the problem. I can break down complex issues into simple, understandable concepts and language so that the customers can understand what I am saying. I have received customer service awards in the technical area for the last two years.

[C] I have a strong background in customer service. Whether the customer is internal or external, I pride myself on my ability to work with people on problems and solutions. I've been chosen for the Customer Service of the Month Award every quarter for the last two years. I always try to give customers my full attention when they call, even when they are complaining or angry.

> **TIP** A good way to prepare for the "strengths" question is to do an assessment of what you have to offer. This means not only your knowledge-based skills (experience and education) but also the skills that are used in almost any job—transferable skills such as communication skills, time management skills, and problem-solving skills.

ANSWERS

The Strongest Answer

[**B**] This is the strongest answer because it gives a broader picture of what you bring to the position, not only providing what is required—technical skills —but also adding extra value by being able to work directly with the customer as well as communicate technical information in simple terms. In today's competitive market, it will be necessary for you to think of your strengths beyond meeting the qualifications. What else can you offer that other candidates cannot? The more skills you can include in your answer, the more information the interviewer will have to judge whether you have what it takes to do the job—and beyond.

The Mediocre Answer

[**C**] This is not as strong an answer as [**B**]. It is a good answer in that it lets the interviewer know that you have a strong ability to work with internal and external customers and work with problems and solutions. This answer would be more effective if you blended in some of the skills that come from your experience or knowledge, such as your industry or product knowledge and how that helps you assist customers.

The Weakest Answer

[**A**] This is a very general answer that could be used for any position. Helping people solve problems is too general a concept to make a good impression on the interviewer. "I love working with people" and "I am a people person" are overused phrases. Be aware of the overuse of any word, and the word *love*, in particular. It is a very "feeling" word and should not be used to excess. An interviewer could sense that you lead with your feelings and may be very sensitive to work with.

RATE YOURSELF

If you chose answer [**B**], give yourself 5 points.

If you chose answer [**C**], give yourself 3 points.

If you chose answer [**A**], give yourself 0 points.

INTERVIEWER'S QUESTION

[6] "What is your greatest weakness?"

Select the strongest answer.

[A] Weaknesses are not something that I dwell on. I am always seeking to improve myself in all areas. For instance, I know I could improve on my patience when working with people who don't work at the same pace as I do. That was something that used to bother me, but as I gain experience and knowledge, what I have found works best is to help the members of the team who are having problems. That way I can move projects forward instead of being frustrated and doing nothing.

[B] You could say that I am a bit of a perfectionist. I am a person who likes to get the job done correctly the first time. One thing that really gets to me, and that I can become very frustrated over, is when other people's work affects my ability to do my job correctly. I've been working on trying to be more understanding and finding out what the problem is before I pass judgment. I recognize that some people are just slow, which is one thing; but they also make mistakes, and that is not tolerable.

[C] My weakness is that I work too hard. I am one of those people who just won't stop until the work is done. Because of the workload, I have to work many evenings and weekends so that projects meet deadlines. I've been told that I have to work smarter and not harder, but that is not easy for me to do. I am a very determined person, and I want to get that job done—no matter what.

> **TIP** Any trait taken to extreme becomes a fault. "I am very determined" could be interpreted as being stubborn and not flexible or adaptable.

ANSWERS

The Strongest Answer

[**A**] This answer is the strongest because it comes across as being very sincere and honest. Some forethought was put into the answer, and that is something you should do in expectation of this question—before the interview. This answer also shows a self-awareness of a need to improve and the action steps that are necessary to work through the issue.

The Mediocre Answer

[**B**] This is not a bad answer. However, the interviewer could become concerned that you are a perfectionist, and that could cause a problem. Avoid mentioning personality traits that would be difficult to change. In answering this question, it is best to demonstrate something you are working on to improve your weakness: "I'm working on changing my behavior by taking management classes and doing yoga."

The Weakest Answer

[**C**] This is a very trite answer and should be avoided. "Working too hard" is a concept that even the cartoons have had some fun with. An interviewer might be concerned about whether you are working hard because of the workload or because of poor work habits.

RATE YOURSELF

If you chose answer [**A**], give yourself 5 points.

If you chose answer [**B**], give yourself 3 points.

If you chose answer [**C**], give yourself 0 points.

INTERVIEWER'S QUESTION

[7] "When have you been most motivated?"

Select the strongest answer.

[A] It was at my previous job where I worked directly with customers and their problems. What I liked was solving problems and helping people. Sometimes it was difficult because of the people constantly complaining and being upset with me. I would try not to take it personally, but I'll admit there were times when it was a challenge. What motivated me was when customers took the time to tell me they appreciated the service.

[B] Last year I was assigned to work with a team, and we had to brainstorm about a product that was not being received well by the consumers. I would wake up in the morning thinking of creative ways to overcome our problem. What was great about this project was the team I was working with. The team really worked together and supported one another. We did a lot of thinking outside the box and came up with creative solutions. It was so successful and rewarding.

[C] I'm pretty motivated all the time. I feel really good about solving problems. I like the challenge of a new problem and the chance to think of solutions. I'm really unmotivated when all I have are pieces of someone else's problem to clean up. I like taking a project from the beginning to the end. I work best when I can take charge of a problem and work through the challenges.

ANSWERS

The Strongest Answer

[**B**] This is the strongest answer because it is the most specific. You can get a strong sense of the enthusiasm and energy behind the motivation and satisfaction. It clearly states that the people and the team are what motivated you. When people are motivated and enthusiastic about what they are doing, they generally perform at a higher level. Interviewers look for enthusiasm and energy in your answers to see what you will bring to the team. Think about the time when you were last motivated. How did it feel? Why?

The Mediocre Answer

[**A**] This answer tends to emphasize the negative aspects of the job almost as much as the motivating or positive side of the job. While it's nice to be appreciated and acknowledged, there are times when no one seems to care whether you are giving good customer service or not—people just want to complain. That's when you have to self-motivate based on your energy toward solving problems and helping others. That would impress the interviewer more than being acknowledged.

The Weakest Answer

[**C**] This is the weakest of the three answers because almost anyone could say these things. This answer also takes a negative turn when it begins to focus on being "unmotivated." Since that was not the question, it is not necessary to volunteer information that might be interpreted as complaining about mundane tasks. This answer also describes the job the way you want it to be. You may talk yourself right out of an offer if you are too specific about your wants. You may sound inflexible—not a good thing if you are asked to take over others' projects in the middle.

RATE YOURSELF

If you chose answer [**B**], give yourself 5 points.

If you chose answer [**A**], give yourself 3 points.

If you chose answer [**C**], give yourself 0 points

INTERVIEWER'S QUESTION

[8] "How would your coworkers describe your personality?"

Select the strongest answer.

[A] I think that they would tell you that I am a high-energy person who is a hard worker. They would also say that I am a quick learner and that I adapt well. I am known for meeting deadlines, and I have the ability to get along well with people. I think that they like my upbeat attitude and sense of humor that keep the department's morale up.

[B] I have had actual feedback from my coworkers during a training seminar. What they had to say is how motivating I am as a team player. They liked my energy and speed for getting things done. I found out that I have a reputation for being reliable at meeting deadlines. They all thanked me for my "whatever it takes to get the job done" attitude and for my motivating spirit.

[C] I'm really not sure what they would say. It would really depend on whom you talked with. I think I am known as a problem solver who is a whiz at analyzing data and transforming the data into useful information. I know my strength is my ability to convert complex details into simple, understandable language. Every company I have worked at has appreciated my ability to save time and money by coming up with solutions.

TIP Even if this question is not asked, it is a good idea to think about what your coworkers would say about you. Third-party endorsements can be very powerful.

ANSWERS

The Strongest Answer

[**B**] This is the strongest answer not only because of the feedback received but because of the confidence and ease in relaying what others had to say. One of the biggest mistakes you can make in an interview is to not talk about your good qualities. This is not the time to be modest. The answer describes your personality through the eyes of your coworkers—of you having a great attitude and a "whatever it takes to get the job done" work ethic. The endorsement from your fellow workers about your ability to be a "team player" is worth far more than anything you can say about yourself.

The Mediocre Answer

[**A**] There is nothing in this answer that makes you unique. If you compare the words in answer [**B**] with those in answer [**A**], you will notice that they basically say the same thing. The difference is the way the information is presented. The terms used in this answer are trite. A high percentage of people would answer with "hard worker." If you do say you are a hard worker, it would be a stronger answer if you referred to a time when you worked above and beyond what was called for: "I often work 10-hour days." Overall this answer needs some punch.

The Weakest Answer

[**C**] This answer refers more to skills than to your personality. It has a strong focus on analytical problem solving but is one-dimensional. By answering the question about what your coworkers would say and adding some personality traits that are more transferable, such as team player, you would give a better, more well-rounded picture of yourself. Any interviewer would want to know more about how you saved time and money at every company that you worked for, but this isn't the best place to talk about that.

RATE YOURSELF

If you chose answer [**B**], give yourself 5 points.

If you chose answer [**A**], give yourself 3 points.

If you chose answer [**C**], give yourself 0 points.

INTERVIEWER'S QUESTION

[9] "Have you ever been fired?"

Select the strongest answer.

[A] Yes. When I accepted my last job, it was primarily because I had a good rapport with my boss. After I was there six months, she left the company. From the very beginning it was clear that my new boss and I were going to be at odds. We just had different personality types. She kept changing the rules. One day she would want it this way, and the next day she'd want it another way. This woman was really overbearing in her management approach. One day she called me in and told me I was fired, with no explanation. She just fired me!

[B] Yes. One of the employees who reported to me made a costly mistake that caused the company to lose a great deal of money. Because I was his boss, we were both fired. At first I did not think this was fair. I now realize that the man was under my supervision and that it was on my shift, and I take full responsibility for what happened. I learned the hard way that as a supervisor I am responsible for the actions of those under me. I have put the incident behind me and am looking forward to moving on to new opportunities.

[C] Yes. I made a mistake in judgment that went against company policy and was fired. I'm not proud of what I did and was hard on myself about the mistake, but I also learned a lot from the incident. There is no point holding on to the past. I will be more careful about my actions in the future. I am ready for a second chance and know that I will be a better employee because of this experience.

> **TIp** People get fired every day. They move on and get new jobs. No matter what the circumstances, it is best to put it behind you. Deal with your feelings about the firing before the interview by scripting a statement that you feel comfortable with. It is important that you display confidence and not get emotional when you talk about this incident.

ANSWERS

The Strongest Answer

[**B**] This is the strongest answer because of the honesty and wisdom of accepting things that are out of your control and taking responsibility. Dealing with your situation with yourself before the interview will keep you from bringing old baggage into the interview. Being able to look the interviewer in the eye and admitting that you made a mistake is not easy, but it may pay off in the long run.

The Mediocre Answer

[**C**] This answer is straightforward and truthful. Laying the truth on the table is a better way of handling the situation than is lying, because one lie leads to another. The way you deliver this answer will be as important as the answer itself. You broke company policy. Some employers will not take a chance on you once you've been fired. However, there will be those who appreciate your honesty and sincerity and may see this as an honorable trait. When you lie in an interview or on an application, there is always the chance you will be found out and may end up being escorted out the door. Don't take the chance.

The Weakest Answer

[**A**] This is the weakest answer because the blame is put on someone else. Even though this was out of your control and you feel you didn't deserve to be fired, it is not a good idea to berate management. It is best to say that when the boss who hired you left, the position changed and it was no longer a good fit with your values and goals. The new boss and you were very different, and it was decided the relationship was not working and you were let go. If you are questioned further, you can say that in retrospect you should have left before the problems occurred and saved everyone a lot of grief.

RATE YOURSELF

If you chose answer [**B**], give yourself 5 points.

If you chose answer [**C**], give yourself 3 points.

If you chose answer [**A**], give yourself 0 points.

INTERVIEWER'S QUESTION

[10] "I see you have been out of work for some time. Why has it taken you so long to find a job?"

Select the strongest answer.

[A] Because the job market is so tight, it hasn't been easy to get a job. I have been in a job search the entire time. I did all the right things, like networking and going to job clubs and meetings. I know the competition for certain jobs is fierce. I did take advantage of the opportunity of the time off to take some online classes and a few short courses. I now feel up-to-date and prepared to find the right opportunity.

[B] The competition is very strong right now, but I am actively seeking employment with the right company. I have an excellent background with five years of experience in this industry and knowledge of several software programs. I know there are a lot of other people out there with similar skills, but what sets me apart from the masses is my ability to relate to and work with a wide range of customers. Having the combination of technical skills and people skills has helped me advance.

[C] I have been consulting, coaching, and volunteering during my time off in various venues. I will not accept just any job offer. As you know, jobs are very scarce right now, and unemployment is at an all-time high. My next job has to be a mutual fit for the organization and for me. My compensation and benefits package will take care of itself, but the opportunity to succeed is the most important factor that needs to be met.

> **TIP** Always focus on what you have and can bring to the job—not on what you don't have. Some people are so focused on their problems that they almost broadcast the negative information to the interviewer.

ANSWERS

The Strongest Answer

[B] This is the most honest answer. It also deflects the question and focuses on what you have to offer, especially what separates you from all the other people applying for this job. Talking about what you can bring to the job, not what you have gone through to get to this interview, is a good technique. Many people tend to focus on what they don't have (a degree or years of experience) instead of focusing on what they do have. Always focus on what you have and can bring to the job—not on what you don't have.

The Mediocre Answer

[A] This is a fairly good answer because it explains what you have been doing in the time you've been unemployed. But it sounds a bit like whining—"I did all the right things, and it still didn't work." It could benefit from some information about you and what you have to offer. Talk more about being up-to-date and any skills you developed that make you ready to go. More details would make this a stronger answer.

The Weakest Answer

[C] This is the weakest answer. It starts off well but then goes downhill by sounding inflexible about the job you are seeking. While it is a good idea to know what you want and are willing to take, you don't have to "demand" it during the interview. This answer also talks about compensation and benefits before it is time to bring those subjects up. Talk about benefits and compensation when asked, or you may talk yourself out of the interview and a possible job offer.

RATE YOURSELF

If you chose answer [B], give yourself 5 points.

If you chose answer [A], give yourself 3 points.

If you chose answer [C], give yourself 0 points.

INTERVIEWER'S QUESTION

[11] "What experience do you have that qualifies you for this position?"

Select the strongest answer.

[A] My experience is a good match with the qualifications needed for this position. I meet all your requirements and then some. I think I could bring added value to this position through my understanding and knowledge of international business in Asian countries. Speaking the language and understanding the cultural norms would be a tremendous asset in negotiations and dealings with companies from those countries.

[B] I know I could do this job. I have the skills and experience necessary to succeed here. I want to work for this company, and I feel that this position would be an opportunity and a challenge for me. I am a person who likes to be challenged, and I also intend to continue to grow and learn new skills. I am strong at solving problems using analytical data. I like working on a team and contributing to solutions.

[C] With six years of experience working in the electronics industry, I have worked on the types of systems required for this job. My strength is my leadership skills. I have supervised technicians and testers on a 24/7 schedule. If you asked my staff members about me, they would tell you that I was there when they needed me. I am very adaptable and have worked as many as 70 hours in a week so that we could meet a deadline.

ANSWERS

The Strongest Answer

[**C**] This is clearly the strongest answer. The answer gives a broad picture of you and illustrates how your skills would fill the interviewer's needs. It gives examples of strengths in the area of technology and leadership skills (which are considered transferable skills) and shows your willingness to do whatever it takes to get the job done. The "third-party endorsement" from the people who have worked with you is very helpful. Speaking through others' comments is a strong technique to use when you are answering questions.

The Mediocre Answer

[**A**] This answer has its strong points, but it does not present as good an overall picture as answer [**C**] does. Any time you can speak of bringing "added value" to a company, whether through languages, people skills, or the ability to do something that most candidates cannot, you should sell it as a strong point. Depending on how important your value is to the position, this could make the difference in your being the chosen candidate.

The Weakest Answer

[**B**] This answer focuses too much on what the job can do for you. The emphasis is best placed on what you can do for the company. This answer would be stronger if it gave specific information about the years of experience and the types of problems solved.

RATE YOURSELF

If you chose answer [**C**], give yourself 5 points.

If you chose answer [**A**], give yourself 3 points.

If you chose answer [**B**], give yourself 0 points.

INTERVIEWER'S QUESTION

[12] "How would your current or last boss describe your job performance?"

Select the strongest answer.

[A] Unfortunately, my last boss and I had very different personalities, and sometimes this resulted in conflicts. I think he would tell you that I was above all a professional in all my dealings with customers, internal and external. He also would tell you that I was reliable and met all my deadlines.

[B] She would tell you that I was her "right-hand man." She would make the decisions, and I did the background and technical work—she relied on me to do all the calculations and data input on projects. I kept her on track when she was running behind schedule, and I jumped in when she needed a hand. She would tell you that I was still her friend even though it's been five years since we worked together.

[C] He would tell you that I have excellent skills working with all kinds of people. He nominated me for an in-service award for my excellent customer service work within the company. He treated me with respect and gave me the feedback I needed to learn and grow in my job. He also would tell you that I was very dependable and could be trusted with confidential information.

ANSWERS

The Strongest Answer

[**B**] This is the stronger answer because it gives a clear picture of the way you work with authority: supportive and responsible. This answer informs the interviewer about your technical skills and abilities as well as your flexibility and willingness. It also speaks of the relationship you built with your boss. Not all jobs end with personal relationships, but if you can quote your boss or mention something positive that a boss said in a performance review, it will strengthen your answer.

The Mediocre Answer

[**C**] This is an acceptable answer but is not as strong as answer [**B**] because it is not as specific. It points out that you have good communication and people skills as well as your being dependable and meeting deadlines, which is good, but it would benefit from an example. The fact that you were nominated for an award is definitely worth mentioning and would benefit from some specifics.

The Weakest Answer

[**A**] This is a weak answer. It's best to avoid talking about differences in a negative way. Although this answer does not really bad-mouth the employer, it points out that there was a problem. The interviewer's concern would be that you did not get along well with your bosses. The answer does have a positive slant because it talks about being professional and meeting deadlines. A good interviewer would probe further and find out the nature of the conflicts. It's best to offer additional information when asked for it, but you don't necessarily have to volunteer to talk about problems.

RATE YOURSELF

If you chose answer [**B**], give yourself 5 points.

If you chose answer [**C**], give yourself 3 points.

If you chose answer [**A**], give yourself 0 points.

INTERVIEWER'S QUESTION

[13] "What do you know about this company?"

Select the strongest answer.

[A] I've done research on the company and checked out the mission statement and what you stand for. I was impressed with your values statement and how you view collaborative teamwork. I am very familiar with your products and the companies you are competing against. I looked up the backgrounds of your two founders and traced their careers and successes. I know that your current stock price is down but that you have a new product in the wings. Above all, I know you are a company that I am very interested in joining.

[B] My interest in this company began when I was in college and did a research paper on companies and stocks. I have followed the progress of the company: the ups and the downs. I know that there are currently some deals in the works that may change the makeup of the company as well as its standing in the industry. I have targeted this company as the place where I want to spend my career.

[C] When I found the posting on the Internet, I wasn't really familiar with the company. I began asking friends and colleagues what they knew about the company. They all had really positive things to say about working for this company. I have heard that this company really treats its employees well and that the benefits here are top of the line.

TIP There's no excuse for not doing research or at least checking out the company's website. Give yourself a competitive edge by doing your homework and researching the company before taking the interview.

ANSWERS

The Strongest Answer

[**A**] This is the strongest answer because of the skills demonstrated while not only researching the company but digging deeper for information about the founders, the competition, future products, and stock. This answer provides information and knowledge beyond what was on the website.

The Mediocre Answer

[**B**] This is not a bad answer. There is enthusiasm for the company and a history of research. It is good to know the direction that the company is heading. What this answer lacks is details about the company, the competition, and the company's standing in the industry. All that information can be found by searching online or at the public library.

The Weakest Answer

[**C**] This is the weakest answer because it does not provide any facts to talk about. Unfortunately, it's not unusual for candidates to lack information about the company. At the very least, a visit to the company website is essential. Relying on the "word" from friends and colleagues is not as good as doing research. This answer also focuses on the "benefits" of working for the company, not on the company itself.

RATE YOURSELF

If you chose answer [**A**], give yourself 5 points.

If you chose answer [**B**], give yourself 3 points.

If you chose answer [**C**], give yourself 0 points.

INTERVIEWER'S QUESTION

[14] "Have you ever had a deadline that you missed? Why did you miss it?"

Select the strongest answer.

[A] No, I've never missed a deadline. I pride myself on meeting deadlines.

[B] Actually, I have never missed a deadline, but there was a time I could have missed several deadlines if I hadn't been as organized as I am. At the time, I was going to school, my wife had just had a baby, and I had just taken on a new responsibility that added about 20 hours to the job I already had. Fortunately, I was able to make a spreadsheet and compartmentalize time so that I met all my obligations. I missed a bit of sleep, and I lost some weight—which was a good thing—but I got through a very trying time with flying colors. My boss was amazed at what I accomplished. The trick was to stay focused and organized.

[C] I did miss a few deadlines in the beginning of this year, but it really wasn't my fault. I work with a team of other representatives, and they aren't as dependable as I am about deadlines. When they didn't provide me with what I needed for the project, I missed the deadline. I really don't have much tolerance for people who don't take deadlines seriously. I am one of those people who will do whatever it takes to meet a deadline.

ANSWERS

The Strongest Answer

[**B**] This is the strongest answer because it states that deadlines could have been missed—as with almost all deadlines—but because of your ability to plan and organize, you met even the toughest deadline. It is not always necessary to have an exact match to the question asked—about missing a deadline—but it is necessary to tell the interviewer what he or she wants to know: can you meet deadlines under pressure? This answer says, "Yes, I can. And let me tell you how I do that."

The Mediocre Answer

[**C**] This answer becomes a weak answer because it puts the blame on others. If there are others who affected your meeting a deadline, you will have to include any attempts you made at taking the initiative to help the project along. The answer sounds like you sat back and waited for the others to provide you with what you needed and just gave up. This answer also doesn't make you sound like a team player who is willing to do whatever it takes. You say that—but you don't show that.

The Weakest Answer

[**A**] This is the weakest answer because it does not take the statement further. "No" is not a good answer. In fact, a good rule is "Never answer a question with a one-word answer." Take the opportunity to tell the interviewer why you pride yourself on meeting deadlines. How do you do it? When you say you "never" missed a deadline, it may sound too good to be true. The interviewer wants to know more about how you have been so successful. Did you work all hours of the night? Did you plan and organize? Did you put your personal life on hold? Or maybe you've never had a tight deadline where you've had to reach out and go above and beyond to meet a deadline. Be sure you answer the complete question asked by the interviewer: "Why?"

RATE YOURSELF

If you chose answer [**B**], give yourself 5 points.

If you chose answer [**C**], give yourself 3 points.

If you chose answer [**A**], give yourself 0 points.

INTERVIEWER'S QUESTION

[15] "What can you do for us that the other candidates can't?"

Select the strongest answer.

[A] I have a strong passion to do this job and do it well. What this job means to me is working for one of the best companies in the field. I really want the challenge that your job offers, and I am willing to do whatever it takes to get this job. I think my energy and enthusiasm are what I bring to the job. Of course, I have the skills and requirements of the job and have had success in this type of job before. But this is the best job I've applied for.

[B] I'm not sure I can answer this question. I am sure there are other people who could do this job. However, I believe that my extensive experience with one of the most prestigious companies in this industry, along with my ability to proactively initiate processes and develop new solutions to old problems, in addition to my technical skills and ability to learn new systems quickly, makes me an ideal candidate.

[C] What I have to bring to this position is over six years working in this industry. I also have my education and training that qualify me as a match. What makes me stand out as a perfect candidate is my ability to solve problems quickly—even working under pressure with tight deadlines. If you ask people who have worked with me, they would tell you that I high a high work ethic and am known for my reliability. At the same time, anyone who knows me would tell you that I have a fun sense of humor that helps us all get through tough situations and builds camaraderie.

ANSWERS

The Strongest Answer

[**C**] This is the strongest answer because it answers the question. It is always smart to have in mind what you bring to any job. This should include your education and training; your area of expertise (an area you are very knowledgeable about); your strength; and some information about you as a person—your personality—especially through your team members' eyes, essentially a third-party endorsement. If you were choosing a candidate, wouldn't it be a plus if the person had a sense of humor that helped get him or her through tough times? You might be surprised that employers see this kind of employee as an upbeat person. Of course, if you don't have a sense of humor, then don't say anything like that—it wouldn't be real or you.

The Mediocre Answer

[**B**] This answer gets off to a bad start. While it's true that you don't know who your competitors are, you don't want to give them "air time." When you say, "I am sure there are other people who could do this job," it doesn't say much for your confidence in yourself and the fact that you can do it better than they could and are therefore the best candidate. The answer gives the information about what you have to offer but does it all in one swoop. This answer needs some breathing space. It would be a stronger answer if you took each quality, one at a time, and talked more about it. These are your areas of strength, not a laundry list of items.

The Weakest Answer

[**A**] While this answer is full of "passion" and enthusiasm, it does not address why you are more qualified than the other candidates—and that was the question. The fact that you want to work for the company and want a challenge doesn't really sell you as the most outstanding candidate. There is a place to show passion and enthusiasm, but it really doesn't work here. This answer almost buries the skills and requirements in all that enthusiasm. Think about what you can do for the company, not what it can do for you.

RATE YOURSELF

If you chose answer [**C**], give yourself 5 points.

If you chose answer [**B**], give yourself 3 points.

If you chose answer [**A**], give yourself 0 points.

INTERVIEWER'S QUESTION

[16] "In what ways has your current or last job prepared you to take on more responsibility?"

Select the strongest answer.

[A] I have had extensive experience working with customers in my last job. In the beginning I had to learn to deal with people who were very frustrated and wanted to take their feelings out on me. I have to admit that in the beginning it really would get to me when someone was being nasty and rude. Since that time, I've taken some training courses on selling and human behavior that have helped immensely. I needed that experience to be able to move forward to a job like this one.

[B] My current job is really not a good fit for me. I am overqualified and somewhat bored. I took the job knowing that I could do it without much of a stretch. The job before this one was a real "burnout" type of environment, and I needed a job that was kind of low key. I am now ready to move forward and give my all to this job. I know I could do this job and bring added value to the department.

[C] My last job was a great stepping-stone for me to take on the new challenges this job will provide. I had to deal with all kinds of situations and people in my last job. After five years in that job, I am ready for some new challenges in a new industry. I know I am ready to move up and would be good at this job because I have the patience needed to deal with difficult people.

ANSWERS

The Strongest Answer

[A] This is the strongest answer because it clearly gives an example of growth and experience. It also talks about training and development to get an understanding beyond the job itself. This is a good example of showing how your past experience is an indicator of your future success.

The Mediocre Answer

[C] This is not a bad answer, but it focuses on "what's in it for me." Most people want "new challenges" in the next job. When too much focus is on the challenge, it takes away from what you bring to the job. The bottom line to the interview process is what you can bring to this company from your past experiences and successes.

The Weakest Answer

[B] This answer has all the indicators of a person who suffered from burnout and took any job just to survive. The interviewer might have reason to be concerned that if it happened before, it can happen again. It is best not to talk about the negatives of any job. Put the focus on the experience and skills you can bring to the new position: "I can bring added value to the job because of my past experience of working in fast-paced environments and still meeting deadlines."

RATE YOURSELF

If you chose answer [A], give yourself 5 points.

If you chose answer [C], give yourself 3 points.

If you chose answer [B], give yourself 0 points.

INTERVIEWER'S QUESTION

[17] "What do you value most in a team?"

Select the strongest answer.

[A] I've worked with a wide variety of people, and the ones who are of most value to me are those who are dependable. One of my pet peeves is to hand off something and find out that it was never taken care of. I don't understand how some people keep their jobs when they can't be depended on to complete the job.

[B] I really value teams who are supportive and are willing to do whatever it takes. A project at my last company really put my team to the test when one of the members had an accident and had to take time off. Even though we each had our own deadlines, we all jumped in to fill the gap when it occurred. It meant two additional long weekends, but we had a common goal. We were able to meet the deadline and feel good about helping someone with a problem.

[C] I value communication skills in any work I do, but in particular when I work with teams. I think it is essential for all the team members to be able to express themselves in a clear manner and be able to listen and follow directions. It's when communications break down that there is no team. It's all about communicating and relating with one another.

ANSWERS

The Strongest Answer

[**B**] This is the strongest answer because it gives a clear example that backs up your opinion. The answer is secondary to the message it conveys. Teamwork means getting along and working together—supporting each other whatever it takes.

The Mediocre Answer

[**A**] This answer could be viewed as a complaining or negative answer. Being dependable is an important trait, but the answer would be stronger if it were phrased in a more positive manner: "I value dependability from teammates because it means the work gets completed and everyone benefits." Leave negative thoughts and comments at home when you are going to an interview.

The Weakest Answer

[**C**] This answer takes on a life of its own and goes down a different path. The answer deals more with effective communication than with "the value of a teammate." The answer is not a wrong answer, because communication skills are very desirable. It just doesn't relate to the question being asked. Always focus on the question asked and address the question.

RATE YOURSELF

If you chose answer [**B**], give yourself 5 points.

If you chose answer [**A**], give yourself 3 points.

If you chose answer [**C**], give yourself 0 points.

INTERVIEWER'S QUESTION

[18] "What are the most important things for you in any job or company?"

Select the strongest answer.

[A] I look for a company that is growth oriented, a place that is secure, where I can grow with the company. There are so many changes going on in the industry, and I am seeking a company that has grown with the trends and technology of today. I want to work for a company that has a solid reputation and foundation. I look for jobs where there has been low turnover because that usually is an indicator of the way people are treated and the benefits they are given.

[B] The number one thing that I look for in a job is the opportunity it allows. To have a chance to work on something really interesting that might make a difference in people's personal or professional lives is my idea of job satisfaction. I don't mean that I want to save the world, but if I can contribute to a company and the goal of that company, I know I can find satisfaction.

[C] The first thing I look for is job satisfaction. What I mean by that is a feeling that my work is of importance in some way to the bottom line or the bigger scheme of things. I also look for jobs that have advancement opportunities. I want to grow with the company. Last, I would like to enjoy my coworkers and have some fun. I spend a lot of time at my job and want it to be a good experience.

> **TIp** Job ads and postings are gifts given to you by the employer. This is the employer's wish list of the qualities it is seeking in a candidate. If you do a comparison between what the employer is looking for and what you have to offer or what you want in a job, you will have an idea whether this is a good match for you. If the job is not a good match, you might want to reconsider applying.

ANSWERS

The Strongest Answer

[**C**] This is the strongest answer because it seems genuine. It offers a broader sweep of values than the other answers do. Job satisfaction is among the top values of most candidates. Because you explain what job satisfaction means to you, the interviewer has a better idea of your career interests. Read through the job description or visit the company's website to determine what values are important at this company. If your values are in line with the company's values, this is an opportunity to let the interviewer know that you will fit in and enjoy working there.

The Mediocre Answer

[**B**] This is not a bad answer, but it may come across as a bit too idealistic or "canned." It's like answering that you want world peace. It is a good idea to be interested in the company's bigger picture and to be a part of that picture, but you would sound more well rounded and realistic if you mentioned a few values that were broader based, such as teamwork, authenticity, balance, or customer satisfaction.

The Weakest Answer

[**A**] This is the weakest answer because it is focused on security and what you will gain if you get this job. No company or organization can guarantee security in today's world of change; that is an unrealistic goal. Asking about turnover is a good idea, but don't state it as one of your criteria in an interview.

RATE YOURSELF

If you chose answer [**C**], give yourself 5 points.

If you chose answer [**B**], give yourself 3 points.

If you chose answer [**A**], give yourself 0 points.

INTERVIEWER'S QUESTION

[19] "How do you stay current and informed about industry trends and technology?"

Select the strongest answer.

[A] I do all the standard things. I read online newspapers. I research the Internet for information on the industry. I read industry journals, and I belong to local networking organizations. I am also a member of a professional organization and attend meetings when I can to network and stay in touch. I really like what I do, and so it is interesting to me to learn and keep current with the ever-changing world we live in.

[B] I actually have a routine to keep up-to-date with industry trends and news. I read online newsletters and the *Business Times* every morning, and I watch CNBC, Reuters, and Bloomberg TV to learn about current events. There are also networking groups on LinkedIn, and I have a list of what I consider good blogs worth reading. I also attend trade shows and seminars and take training presented by the technology companies whenever it is available. I believe that if you don't keep up with the social media trends, you will get left behind.

[C] There isn't much time left in the day after my long work hours. I have been working extremely long hours for the past year. My busy life does not allow for much more than watching the evening news to catch up with the latest happenings. I always read my company's newsletters and the bulletins on the website to stay in touch with what's happening in the company. I do some social media interacting—but not on a regular basis.

ANSWERS

The Strongest Answer

[**B**] This answer is the most up-to-date and therefore strongest for the answer to this question. Depending on what industry you work in, your answer may not be as technology oriented. There is no denying that social media is important and is changing our day-to-day thinking and interactions, and letting the interviewer know that you are "in the know" and engaging in social outreach will be important.

The Mediocre Answer

[**A**] This answer has a very natural, relaxed tone to it, and yet it covers every possible base and states that you are a person who is "out there" and informed. By being involved in groups and organizations, you are constantly widening your network, which is the number one way to get a job. The answer would benefit from more specifics. Of course, in your interview you'd give the specific names of newsletters and organizations.

The Weakest Answer

[**C**] Although this might be a "real" answer, this is not the strongest position to be in as an informed person. Regardless of the position you hold in a company, staying informed about the latest trends and issues is crucial for job success. The world of technology is moving too fast to be ignored as a way of staying in contact with others and industry and financial news.

RATE YOURSELF

If you chose answer [**B**], give yourself 5 points.

If you chose answer [**A**], give yourself 3 points.

If you chose answer [**C**], give yourself 0 points.

INTERVIEWER'S QUESTION

[20] "Do you work well under pressure?"

Select the strongest answer.

[A] Absolutely. I think most clearly when rushed to meet deadlines. I am very adaptable and can act quickly when I have to. I think my efficiency really shines when I am asked to prepare reports in a few hours. Because I am always very organized and know where information is stored, I can produce almost on demand. I have a high attention to detail, and that helps keep the quality up even when I am rushed.

[B] Most of the time. I have worked for companies when pressure was the norm. I am one of those people who don't get rattled easily, and so I don't take it personally. I do what I can, and that's all I can do. The turnover at the company was pretty high because most people burned out and left. I feel good about the fact that I stayed for several years, and I think my manager knew not to push too hard or I might leave as well.

[C] I am a person who likes to plan ahead and get things done ahead of schedule. That's how I handle pressure, by being prepared and organized. I really don't appreciate others not planning ahead and expecting me to drop everything and get them whatever it is that they need—immediately. I think the people that worked with me knew that was not my style and didn't do that to me very often. If they did give it to me, I would always get it done for them.

ANSWERS

The Strongest Answer

[**A**] This is the strongest answer because it is upbeat and assuring that this person knows how to deal with the stress and pressure. At the same time, this answer weaves in quite a few skills and traits: adaptable, efficient, organized, flexible, attention to detail, concern about quality. Any time you can work in some of your skills or traits, it will continue to remind the interviewer that you have those skills by creating a pattern of behavior.

The Mediocre Answer

[**B**] This answer does show an ability to handle pressure—and over a long period of time. While it is good not to get rattled, it could be interpreted as not caring by not getting involved. The answer does demonstrate a sense of loyalty for staying when turnover is high—for whatever reason. It sounds like management might be glad to have a long-term employee and has learned to back off and leave the person be. Yet this probably is not the best thing to talk about in an interview for a new job.

The Weakest Answer

[**C**] This answer has attitude. It's a good thing to plan ahead and get things done on schedule, but there are times when that is not possible—or when an emergency of some kind comes up. Not appreciating others' lack of planning might not go over well in an interview, especially if the interviewer is one of those last-minute people. It does have a redeeming ending when you say that if you get something like that, you would do whatever it takes to get it done.

RATE YOURSELF

If you chose answer [**A**], give yourself 5 points.

If you chose answer [**B**], give yourself 3 points.

If you chose answer [**C**], give yourself 0 points.

INTERVIEWER'S QUESTION

[21] "If I asked your coworkers to say three positive things about you, what would they say?"

Select the strongest answer.

[A] They probably would first tell you that I am very knowledgeable about my job and am willing to share my knowledge with them whenever they need help. Second, they would tell you that I have great organizational skills. I plan ahead and meet schedules. The third thing they would tell you is that I know when to laugh. I've learned through experience that you can't take some situations too seriously.

[B] I'm not really sure what they would say. We all work well together but don't have much social interaction. I think they would tell you that I am a hard worker, because I am. I think they would tell you I am a very thoughtful person; at least I try to be. And I think they would say I am a team player. I always try to help others.

[C] That's a difficult question. I think they think I am responsible. I'm always cooperative. I don't gossip or get involved in company politics. On the negative side, some of them think I'm aloof because I don't get involved in the gossip. I am very selective about whom I become friends with at work. I think it is best to keep work on a nonpersonal basis.

ANSWERS

The Strongest Answer

[**A**] This is the strongest answer not only because it offers specific examples but because it provides a mixture of skills and traits—some knowledge-based skills, some general or transferable traits, and some personal traits—that make you a likable person. It's best when you can give a mixture of skills and traits. These are the things that make you different from the next person who comes to interview. Think about what makes you unique: what makes you "rememberable"?

The Mediocre Answer

[**B**] This answer would be stronger if you gave some reasons for the answers, such as "They would tell you I am a very thoughtful person. I always remember everyone's birthday and send a card or a little gift." When you give an example with the statement, it makes more of an impact. Also, avoid the phrase "I think." It makes you appear less confident.

The Weakest Answer

[**C**] This answer is weak because it does not have a positive viewpoint and turns negative at the end. Never volunteer a negative thought about yourself unless you are asked for a weakness. This answer does not give the impression that you are much of a team player. In fact, it could keep you from getting the job if you are going to be part of a team. Among the traits most interviewers look for are the ability to relate to others and communication skills.

RATE YOURSELF

If you chose answer [**A**], give yourself 5 points.

If you chose answer [**B**], give yourself 3 points.

If you chose answer [**C**], give yourself 0 points.

INTERVIEWER'S QUESTION

[22] "How have you contributed to teamwork in your jobs?"

Select the strongest answer.

[A] I consider myself a real team player. I always ask people if I can help them if they have extra work to do. I also make sure that I say "Good morning" when anyone comes in. I am a bit of a cheerleader about things like charitable drives and social events. I know how to relate to people and try to keep up with what's going on. I think my coworkers see me as very social and team oriented and cooperative.

[B] When I was growing up—in high school—I played a lot of sports, and that experience taught me more about team cooperation than anything else I could have learned in a class or by reading a book. In sports you need to rely on one another, and if you don't work together, your team will lose. I have a strong competitive spirit, and so when I can rally the team to do better work, I do—just like I did when I was playing basketball.

[C] When I get a new job, one of the first things I do is to get to know the people who are most connected. This is a good way to build alliances with people whom you can help later on and who become resources who can help you. In several of our projects, we needed the cooperation of the other departments; and because I have built relationships with people all over the company, I have been able to rally support for whatever project we are working on. This has really helped any team I've worked with.

ANSWERS

The Strongest Answer

[**C**] This is the strongest answer because it gets specific about the ways that you contributed to the team. By showing that you are aware of using people as a resource, you show the interviewer that you can be resourceful working through other departments. If this were a behavioral question, it would sound like "Tell me about a time when you contributed to a team," a question you could answer more specifically through a story. This question is open ended, and telling what you have done in the past is a good way to answer the question.

The Mediocre Answer

[**A**] This isn't a bad answer, but it is rather vague about the ability to motivate people in work situations. It really sounds more like a "sunshine" person—which is not a bad thing—but you could strengthen your answer if you talked a bit more about work projects and the things you did to make the team stronger and more cooperative.

The Weakest Answer

[**B**] While a sports analogy is a good way to answer a question about teams, this answer focuses almost exclusively on sports teams. To make it a stronger story, you should show how this learned skill has helped you in your work teams—and how you in turn helped your coworkers by motivating and encouraging them. Even though an example was not asked for, you could give one that demonstrates how what you learned playing sports translates into the office setting.

RATE YOURSELF

If you chose answer [**C**], give yourself 5 points.

If you chose answer [**A**], give yourself 3 points.

If you chose answer [**B**], give yourself 0 points.

INTERVIEWER'S QUESTION

[23] "If I remember only one thing about you, what should that be?"

Select the strongest answer.

[A] I have an unusual hobby that you might remember my mentioning. I collect one-of-a-kind stamps that have printing errors. I have a collection worth thousands of dollars. Finding these stamps is a big challenge.

[B] I can be remembered for my excellent communication skills and experience working with all types of people. I really want to help people. I always try to get along with every person that I work with. It makes for a better work environment if people get along.

[C] I have two skills that are distinctly different but that define my personality. I am a very good pianist and an excellent computer "guy." I'm known for my love of keyboards. You could remember that I have two mindsets—analytical with the computer and creative with the piano.

ANSWERS

The Strongest Answer

[**C**] This is the strongest answer, especially if computer skills are needed for the job. Obviously, you will not always be able to relate your hobbies to your job, but you can see how this would make the interviewer remember you after you finished the interview. The idea is to find something that sets you apart from the other candidates.

The Mediocre Answer

[**A**] This is an interesting answer that would qualify as a "memorable" statement, but it's not as strong as answer [**C**] because it doesn't relate directly to the job. If you can tie your hobby into the job functions, your answer would be stronger. You might say, "I am very determined when it comes to hunting down a stamp that I want. I'm the same way when it comes to solving problems at work." By giving examples of skills you use in your hobby, you can strengthen your answer.

The Weakest Answer

[**B**] The problem with this answer is that it is one that almost anyone could give. There is nothing unique about it. The idea of being good with people and communications is fine, but you will need to expand on the idea to make it stand out. An example: "Because of my excellent communication skills, I am able to break down complex problems into user-friendly concepts. I'm known as the 'word wizard' at work."

RATE YOURSELF

If you chose answer [**C**], give yourself 5 points.

If you chose answer [**A**], give yourself 3 points.

If you chose answer [**B**], give yourself 0 points.

INTERVIEWER'S QUESTION

[24] "What are your salary expectations?"

Select the strongest answer.

[A] My current salary is $50,000. I also have stock options and bonuses and a very generous benefits package. I would like to compare your benefits package before I give you an exact number.

[B] I really need more information about the job and other benefits before I can come up with a figure. I think after I have the facts, we can come to a mutually agreeable figure. Could you share with me the range that you have budgeted for the position?

[C] I'm sure whatever you offer will be a fair amount for a person with my experience and qualifications. I am more interested in working for this company and the opportunity that it allows.

ANSWERS

The Strongest Answer

[**B**] This is the stronger answer because it postpones the conversation until there are more facts available. It also puts the onus on the employer by asking what range has been budgeted. Until you have a thorough understanding of the job responsibilities and the range allowed for a person with your background or experience, you cannot give the interviewer an accurate figure. Don't be surprised if the interviewer pushes back and asks again. In that case, try to use a range versus an exact figure.

The Mediocre Answer

[**C**] This is a nice way of saying, "I trust you to treat me fairly," which could be viewed as somewhat passive or naive. When the time comes, you may be surprised that the company does not make a fair offer because you didn't ask for one. That is when you will have to become more realistic about your salary expectations. One thing to know before you go into the interview is what the going rate is for someone with your experience and qualifications. There are several websites with industry and job salary information.

The Weakest Answer

[**A**] There is a general negotiating rule that states, "Never give out a number first. The person who mentions a figure first loses." When you give a number such as $50,000, you are taking a chance because it may be too high for this position or possibly too low. It is best to get the interviewer to name the number by asking for the "range allowed." If you do your salary homework before the interview, you will know what a reasonable offer is for someone with your experience and qualifications.

RATE YOURSELF

If you chose answer [**B**], give yourself 5 points.

If you chose answer [**C**], give yourself 3 points.

If you chose answer [**A**], give yourself 0 points.

INTERVIEWER'S QUESTION

[25] "Do you have any questions?"

Select the strongest answer.

[A] I would like to know what the bonus situation is and how it is decided who will receive a bonus and who will not. I also would like to know more about payment of the premiums on healthcare insurance.

[B] You have been very thorough in your explanation of what the job entails. I don't have any further questions at this time. I'm sure I would have more questions once I started the job.

[C] One thing that has been talked about during the interview process is the "branding" of your product. Could you tell me what has worked to this point and what you would expect to see done differently?

> **TIP** The best questions come from what you hear during the interview. Pay attention to the questions asked. You can pick up valuable information by listening to what is said and what is not said. Read between the lines and then ask for more information.

ANSWERS

The Strongest Answer

[**C**] This is the strongest answer because it shows that you have been listening and are aware that one of your first projects will be to work on the branding issue. The bottom line of the interviewing process is "What can you do for us?" By asking what has worked and what has not, you demonstrate an ability to listen to the problem, and then you can address what is needed to solve the problem. By listening carefully to what has been said, you will be able to ask questions that are of interest to "them."

The Mediocre Answer

[**A**] Depending on where you are in the interview process, this answer could be appropriate. This would not be a good question to ask in a first interview before any interest is shown. This answer or question, on your part, focuses on what you will get out of working for this company. You will need the information eventually; just wait until the appropriate time to bring it up, such as during a second interview or when it is clear that an offer is pending.

The Weakest Answer

[**B**] This is the most common reply used by candidates—"No, I don't have any questions"—and it is the wrong answer. It is very important that you ask questions to show your interest and let the interviewer know you have been listening. Some managers will ask an interviewer to keep track of the questions asked by the candidate to see where the interest lies. You should focus on what the employer's problem is and what you are expected to do if you get the position.

RATE YOURSELF

If you chose answer [**C**], give yourself 5 points.

If you chose answer [**A**], give yourself 3 points.

If you chose answer [**B**], give yourself 0 points.

Behavioral Interview Questions

This section of the Interview IQ Test focuses on behavioral interview questions. As discussed previously, these types of questions are being used more frequently by all kinds of companies because they allow the interviewer to seek examples of specific skills, knowledge, and experience that the job candidate possesses. You can recognize behavioral interview questions by the wording of the question. A typical behavioral question might start with one of the following:

"Tell me about a time when . . ."

"Can you give me an example of . . . ?"

"Describe a time when . . ."

As soon as you hear the interviewer asking for an example, you will know that he or she wants to hear about a specific time when you actually did what you said you did. In other words, "Prove it; tell me a story." The interviewer is seeking proof that you actually have the background you claim to have on your résumé. The key to answering behavioral questions is to be specific. The more recent and job related the example, the more effective your answer will be.

If you do not have a recent, work-related example to relay, use a volunteer, college, or life experience. The important point is that the example relate in some way to the qualities sought for the job for which you are applying. For instance, if an interviewer asks you for a time when you had a conflict with a coworker, the interviewer probably wants to know how you get along with people—how you communicate with and relate to others.

An important rule to follow regarding behavioral interview questions is to not say anything on your résumé or during the interview that you cannot follow up with an example or a story.

In Part 2 you will learn how to write and tell your own stories in an organized, succinct manner, relaying your experiences and showing the interviewer that you have had such experiences and you could repeat the behaviors again—at this company.

It is now time for the behavioral section of the Interview IQ Test.

The Interview IQ Test: Behavioral Questions

INTERVIEWER'S QUESTION

[26] "Tell me about the biggest project you've worked on from start to finish."

Select the strongest answer.

[A] The company I worked for received a huge order; in fact, it was the biggest order the company ever achieved. The order was for a major client, and the completion of the order would be a major bonus for us—and a revenue stream for the future. Our challenge was a pricing issue. To design what we set out to design became unreasonable because of the cost of materials and labor. After many meetings, we were able to combine some of the features of the product and still satisfy the customer. I never worked harder on a project to meet an unrealistic expectation.

[B] We had a safety project that most of us had little or no experience with before. We really had to pull together and share information and resources to pull this one off. Fortunately, we all got along well and supported one another. We were able to put together this project with a lot of effort. We stayed late and worked weekends for two months. We worked closely with the other departments in the company to make sure we were meeting the customer's needs. The good news is that we were able to get it done. Everybody felt really good about pulling together on this one.

[C] I was in charge of designing the safety program for a huge order received by my last company. The first thing I did was to select three top technicians to work with me. We worked as a team, with each of us assigned a piece of the project. I led the group by coordinating the schedules and making sure all the deadlines were met. I was in constant communication with my team members and was there to troubleshoot as needed. Because of the open communication among the four of us, we were able to complete the project ahead of the shipping date.

ANSWERS

The Strongest Answer

[**C**] This is the strongest answer because it gives a very clear picture, with details of the situation. Even though this was a team situation, the interviewer is able to see your role in solving the problem. By using the pronoun *I*, you give a clearer picture of the skills you used. This example talks about some of the skills you used: leadership, coordinating, follow-through, tracking, communication, problem solving, time management, and troubleshooting.

The Mediocre Answer

[**B**] There is a definite problem with this answer: there are too many *wes* (eight to be exact) and not enough *Is* (none). As the answer stands, the interviewer has no idea what your role was. While it is important to give credit where credit is due, it is also necessary to describe what you did to pull this project together as a team member or leader.

The Weakest Answer

[**A**] This is a weak answer because it puts too much emphasis on the company and the project and not enough on your role. What exactly was your role in this team effort? One of the biggest mistakes candidates make is not saying what their role was. More details of your actions are needed for this to be a strong answer.

RATE YOURSELF

If you chose answer [**C**], give yourself 5 points.

If you chose answer [**B**], give yourself 3 points.

If you chose answer [**A**], give yourself 0 points.

> **TIP** The correct use of the pronouns *I* and *we* in your stories is critical. While it is important to not take credit for something that the team did, it is equally important to give yourself credit for your role in a project. When you use *we* instead of *I*, it is difficult for the interviewer to determine your role.

INTERVIEWER'S QUESTION

[27] "Describe a time when you had to adapt to a new situation."

Select the strongest answer.

[A] I've become quite accustomed to new situations in the IT industry. I have been laid off twice in the last five years. In fact, one of the companies closed the doors as we walked out. I've had to accept the fact that not all start-up companies are going to make it.

[B] My military background has prepared me for this part of any job. When you have been on call day and night and responsible for your unit's safety, you learn to be adaptable and flexible. Being flexible in the service is not only necessary; it is mandatory. I bring that same set of skills and sense of urgency to any job. I do whatever it takes to get the job done.

[C] I was on call 24/7 one weekend, and when the phone rang on Sunday morning, I knew there was a problem. Sure enough, there was a mainframe that went down. The first thing I did was to cancel my plans for the day. I responded to the call within one hour. I teamed up with three technicians to get the system up and running before morning. We each had a responsibility but worked as a unit. We stayed until 2 a.m. When the employees arrived at work that Monday morning, no one was aware there had been a problem. We got high kudos for responding so quickly.

ANSWERS

The Strongest Answer

[**C**] This is the strongest answer because it answers the question with a specific example of adapting to a situation. It allows the interviewer to hear how flexible you are when you describe canceling plans and getting to the scene within an hour. This answer also shows how well you work with others. Your willingness to stay until 2 a.m. should convince the interviewer that you are dedicated to getting the job done.

The Mediocre Answer

[**B**] While this is a good example, it is a mediocre answer because it does not give an example of a specific time. You show that you have a sense of adaptability and that you have experience responding to new and unexpected situations, but what is missing is a specific example to ensure that this is not talk with no action. In other words, can you really do it?

The Weakest Answer

[**A**] This answer doesn't show how you adapted to something that was within your control. It is not a bad answer because it shows that you were able to adapt when you were laid off; but your answer does not say how you adapted to a situation where your actions would have made a difference. This answer is more about accepting and moving on than it is adapting. Anyone can get laid off and adapt to not getting a paycheck, but what you did to take control of a situation is more important.

RATE YOURSELF

If you chose answer [**C**], give yourself 5 points.

If you chose answer [**B**], give yourself 3 points.

If you chose answer [**A**], give yourself 0 points.

INTERVIEWER'S QUESTION

[28] "Tell me about a time when you had to handle a stressful situation."

Select the strongest answer.

[A] That's the way of life in this profession. We always seem to be short-staffed. If you can't handle the stress, you can't succeed as a nurse. We all work as hard as we can and as fast as we can; sometimes, though, that's just not enough. We get complaints and have to deal with it. There have been times where I have had as many as 20 patients and had to handle it. That's just the nature of the game. I'm good at what I do, and I do whatever it takes. There are always shortages and budget problems, and you just have to deal with it. I have the qualities needed to do this job.

[B] There was a time when I was working at a hospital and we were short-staffed because two nurses called in sick. A nurse named Faye and I were the only ones on duty, and we had 28 patients to care for. It was one of those times when everything that could go wrong did: patients were yelling, and one patient fell. Faye and I discussed the situation and did a quick priority check. One thing that we knew would make a difference was our support of each other. We would give each other a little smile or a hand signal from time to time to let the other one know that we were hanging in there. Somehow we got through the night and assisted every patient, but at the time it was very stressful.

[C] I know what it takes to get this job done. I pride myself on staying calm when everything around me is falling apart. I don't like stress, but I know how to deal with it. I just do my work and try to ignore the unpleasant things that take place. I'm paid to do a service, and I do it. We each have our own area of responsibility. I do mine, and I do it well. I get through my shift, and that's the end. I don't take problems home with me.

ANSWERS

The Strongest Answer

[**B**] This is the strongest answer because it provides an example of you being a real team player and handling stressful situations. This reply demonstrates your ability to remain cool and think straight when things are too hot to handle. The skills heard in this example are teamwork, adaptability, the ability to handle pressure, the ability to prioritize, a sense of humor, and the ability to communicate. You can see the power of good storytelling if you are trying to show the interviewer what you have to offer through examples.

The Mediocre Answer

[**A**] This is not the strongest answer, but it does have merit. It does not give a specific example as was asked for in the question. It would be a stronger answer if you expanded it with a specific example. The statement "I have had as many as 20 patients" shows the scope of responsibility; but a specific example would have shown the skills it took to deal with the situation.

The Weakest Answer

[**C**] This is the weakest answer. In addition to sounding negative, it does not address the question about a specific time. This answer has the tone of someone with a defeatist attitude. That may be the way things are, but the answer points out all the negatives of the job and none of the positives. This answer could be interpreted as coming from a person who is burned out or has given up trying to improve the situation.

RATE YOURSELF

If you chose answer [**B**], give yourself 5 points.

If you chose answer [**A**], give yourself 3 points.

If you chose answer [**C**], give yourself 0 points.

INTERVIEWER'S QUESTION

[29] "Your résumé states that you're a hard worker. Can you give me an example of a time when you worked hard?"

Select the strongest answer.

[A] I always try to get the work done on time. Sometimes that means working overtime. Sometimes I can't get all my work done during the day and am willing to stay late to finish up. There have been times when I just couldn't get everything done no matter how hard I worked. I always do my best to meet deadlines, but sometimes you just have to let go. I'd rather do it right and be late than do it wrong and be on time.

[B] I am a very hard worker. I am always punctual and get my work done. The tighter the deadline is, the harder I work. I plan my day so that I'm never late with my work, and I always meet deadlines. If you asked my last boss, he would tell you what a hard worker I am. I do whatever I have to do to get the job done.

[C] In my recent job, my boss had a really important project, and it didn't look like we were going to make the deadline. I volunteered to do some late nights and weekends. My boss and two coworkers worked seven straight days with no time off. My piece of the project was to coordinate all the information and enter the data. It was a real team effort, but we were able to meet the deadline. My boss was extremely pleased, and he rewarded us all for our efforts.

ANSWERS

The Strongest Answer

[C] This is the strongest answer because it gives a specific example of going above and beyond what was expected. Some of the skills that appear in this answer are initiative, teamwork, coordination skills, a great attitude, and a cooperative spirit—and a willingness to make the boss look good.

The Mediocre Answer

[B] This is not as strong an answer as [C]. It provides all the right traits— punctual, conscientious, good attitude—but no examples of using those traits in an actual situation. This answer does benefit from the endorsement from your boss. Bringing the boss into the story is a great way to strengthen the story.

The Weakest Answer

[A] This is the weakest answer because it does not include an example of working hard and emphasizes meeting deadlines, which is not quite the same skill. The interviewer could get the idea that you miss deadlines and have a difficult time keeping up with the workload. This answer needs to emphasize the times you stayed late and the reason why the workload was too big to handle.

RATE YOURSELF

If you chose answer [C], give yourself 5 points.

If you chose answer [B], give yourself 3 points.

If you chose answer [A], give yourself 0 points.

INTERVIEWER'S QUESTION

[30] "Tell me about a time when you had a disagreement or conflict with a boss or coworker."

Select the strongest answer.

[A] In my last job, my boss refused to take action against an employee who was getting away with doing something that went against company policy. I was upset about the situation. I feel that everyone should be treated equally and that it was wrong for this person to get away with something when the rest of us had to conform. I talked to my boss, but that didn't work. I ended up going to human resources and complaining. My boss was unhappy with me for going over his head, but action was taken and the employee was disciplined. My boss eventually got over it.

[B] I'm one of those people who try to get along with everyone. I try to ignore people who have irritating qualities. It's just not worth getting into a snit about it. I try to be as professional as possible when I work. If I get upset, I go for a walk or take a break to get away from the situation. I really don't like confrontation.

[C] There was a coworker who was taking extra time off at lunch and giving me a problem because I was her backup. Rather than let it fester, I asked her if we could talk after work. I explained to her in a nonaccusing manner that there was a problem. She told me that she had been trying to accomplish personal tasks at lunch that were taking longer than expected and that she would stop doing that. She hadn't thought about the impact it was having on my work. Things changed for the better after our discussion.

ANSWERS

The Strongest Answer

[**C**] This is the strongest answer. Communication skills are the most important skills in most jobs. This answer demonstrates an ability to face up to difficult situations and nip the problem before it becomes full blown. The example is somewhat short but does have a beginning, a middle, and an end—the key components for a behavioral story.

The Mediocre Answer

[**A**] This is a good answer because it is a specific example, but it is a bit risky to give an example of a time when you went against your boss. This incident had a positive result, but if you were interviewing with a hiring manager, it might cause some doubt about your ability to be a team player. It would be advisable to stay away from stories that make your boss look weak, especially if you are interviewing with your "future" boss. If you did it before, you can do it again.

The Weakest Answer

[**B**] This isn't a bad answer, but it is somewhat passive, as seen in the statements "I try to ignore people," "If I get upset, I go for a walk," and "I really don't like confrontation." What an interviewer might hear is that you are a person who "stuffs" things and holds them in rather than taking action. Some employees who are passive have a breaking point when they reach their limit and "boil over." This behavior is known as "passive-aggressive." It's all right to be irritated by fellow employees. The issue becomes how you handle the situation—what are your communication and judgment skills.

RATE YOURSELF

If you chose answer [**C**], give yourself 5 points.

If you chose answer [**A**], give yourself 3 points.

If you chose answer [**B**], give yourself 0 points.

INTERVIEWER'S QUESTION

[31] "What was the most difficult problem you've handled? How did you deal with it?"

Select the strongest answer.

[A] One of my strengths is my ability to see a problem through to the end no matter what it takes. I have a high work ethic for myself and always do my job and more. My boss would tell you that I am a really dedicated worker. I have been known to stay until 10 or 11 at night to see a project through to completion. I get a lot of satisfaction when I see a job through.

[B] That would be a time when it was our peak season, and we were behind schedule. We only had two weeks left before the deadline. I took the initiative and gathered the team leaders to talk about the situation. We brainstormed some ideas about how we could meet the customer's deadline. One of my ideas was to divide the project into specific pieces, which isn't the way it was done before. I persuaded them to give it a try. Each person was in charge of a section. I made sure everyone stayed on track by checking with everybody every evening before the close of business. It was a remarkable effort, but we were able to come in under deadline.

[C] This was a time when I was very frustrated because my team was letting me down and there was a good chance that we would not make a certain deadline. I get irritated when someone on the team is not pulling his or her weight. I strongly believe that we are all accountable to ourselves and shouldn't have to have a manager looking over our shoulders to get our work done. I was raised with the ethic of "Work hard to earn your salary, and you will get what you deserve in return."

ANSWERS

The Strongest Answer

[**B**] This answer demonstrates several skills: leadership, creative thinking, problem solving, and follow-through, and it also shows that you are a team player. When the question is answered with a specific example, the interviewer can hear the strong skills demonstrated. Patterns begin to develop, and a picture of the way you work is formed.

The Mediocre Answer

[**A**] The words are there; the example is not. Saying that you can go above and beyond—that you will "see a problem through to the end no matter what it takes"—is stronger when you can describe a time when you did that. This answer brings in a third party—the boss—which strengthens the statement "I have a high work ethic," but it provides no example that substantiates that statement. Behavioral interviewing is about giving specific examples.

The Weakest Answer

[**C**] This is the weakest answer because it "preaches." The question starts out well with the situation but quickly goes into meltdown with each additional sentence. The question was not about hard work. It asked about the most difficult problem you had to handle. Be sure you are answering the question asked—and use specific examples.

RATE YOURSELF

If you chose answer [**B**], give yourself 5 points.

If you chose answer [**A**], give yourself 3 points.

If you chose answer [**C**], give yourself 0 points.

INTERVIEWER'S QUESTION

[32] "Tell me about a time when you had to adapt quickly to a change."

Select the strongest answer.

[A] While working as a salesperson, I decided to run the numbers on a certain food item. What I discovered was that sales were declining. I had to move quickly to come up with a plan to turn the sales around. Using demographics, I discovered that we were off on our target market. I immediately put together a proposal, and within a week we had a new marketing focus to reach the right customers. The new plan included coupons, two-for-ones, and special displays to attract customers. By the end of the month, sales rose significantly. I was rewarded by management for my quick actions.

[B] I actually like change. In fact, I thrive on change. I am a person who can adapt easily to any situation you put me in. I was with one company in which upper management changed three times in one year. I just don't let it get to me. I know how to roll with the punches. The worst thing for me is to not have change. To continue doing the same thing for years would really not be what I want from a job or career. Movement keeps me growing and learning; I like being challenged.

[C] Change is something that happens every day in this industry. A policy difference can make everyone jump, and we have very little power over the situation. That has been one of the most frustrating things about my current job. There were just too many changes, without any thought behind them. I don't want to complain about management, but sometimes the management changed the way we were doing something and then a week later changed it back to the way it had been before. That can be very frustrating for an employee.

> **TIP** It is not a good idea to bad-mouth a former boss or company in an interview. If you need to talk about a negative matter, speak only about the facts.

ANSWERS

The Strongest Answer

[**A**] This is the strongest answer because it gives a very action-oriented example: There was a problem. You moved quickly to solve the problem. The problem was resolved. There is a strong sense of what your role was in the situation. This answer also would be a good reply to a question dealing with problem solving or coming up with a creative idea.

The Mediocre Answer

[**B**] This answer borders on being dangerous because it gives an impression of restlessness. Because you say that change is good but lack of change is deadly for you, the interviewer could get the impression that you aren't going to stick around long, particularly if this is a dead-end job. There is no need to emphasize things that might make the interviewer get the wrong idea of you and your goals.

The Weakest Answer

[**C**] This answer has a negative, whiny tone. It is a bad idea to bad-mouth former employers in an interview. Even if you have had bad experiences at a company, it is best to deal with those feelings before you go to the interview. Nothing good can come of dragging past baggage into the interview with you. In fact, it could be a real turn-off.

RATE YOURSELF

If you chose answer [**A**], give yourself 5 points.

If you chose answer [**B**], give yourself 3 points.

If you chose answer [**C**], give yourself 0 points.

INTERVIEWER'S QUESTION

[33] "Can you give me an example of working in a fast-paced environment?"

Select the strongest answer.

[A] I thrive on fast-paced environments where I am challenged to meet deadlines. The more pressure there is, the better I respond. I have been involved in as many as five projects at the same time, all with tight deadlines. I always learn from each project I accomplish and can apply the new learning to the next project to be more efficient. I have the ability to think very quickly and respond to situations as needed, with a good sense of what is needed. I've never had an assignment when I haven't had success. I have very good organizational and communication skills. I also have great computer skills that can help with the tracking of a project.

[B] When I was a support person in a law office, there was one time when we had to get everything ready for a case and were short-staffed because one of the other support persons was out ill. I took on the responsibility of coordinating all the reports. The first thing I did was sit down with the attorneys involved and ask them to give me an idea of the priorities that they needed to complete their projects. I then put together a task spreadsheet and worked with everyone to keep on track. We worked late into the night: 2 a.m. Instead of being tired, I felt energized throughout the experience. It was really rewarding when we finished the last task and made the deadline. Everyone was surprised at how smoothly it went with all the obstacles I had to work around. I received a nice bonus for my efforts.

[C] We had this project to work on, and it seemed like everything was going wrong. First of all, we had a very tight deadline and were short a staff member. We had handled this type of pressure before, but this was a particularly important case because it was one of our major clients. This case included a lot of visuals, such as charts and graphs and photos. The attorneys were under a lot of pressure, and there was a lot of tension in the office. At one point I just felt like sitting down and crying, but I didn't. I just kept working through the anxiety and tension. I knew that if we didn't get this pulled together in time, there would be a very dissatisfied client. We all worked overtime that weekend, but we completed the job on time.

ANSWERS

The Strongest Answer

[**B**] This is the strongest answer because it provides a very good example of working in a fast-paced environment—which is what the question is about. It also shows a good attitude of pitching in and getting something done. This example points out organizational skills, initiative, leadership, judgment, the ability to communicate, and a willingness to do whatever it takes to get the job done. This story also provides an example of overcoming obstacles.

The Mediocre Answer

[**A**] This answer basically gives the same information that is given in answer [**B**], but without any examples. You say that you "have very good organizational and communications skills." Prove it. Give an example. Anybody can say that he or she is good at any task, but when you give a specific example of a time when you did the task, the interviewer gets a better idea of how you worked in the past—and will consider it as an indicator of future success.

The Weakest Answer

[**C**] This answer does not reveal any of your skills. There is too much emphasis on the problem without an explanation of your role. There are too many *wes* and not enough *Is*. The only direct reference to your behavior is when you talk about how stressed you were: "I just felt like sitting down and crying." The positive is that you said, "but I didn't," which indicates that you are not a quitter and that you have perseverance.

RATE YOURSELF

If you chose answer [**B**], give yourself 5 points.

If you chose answer [**A**], give yourself 3 points.

If you chose answer [**C**], give yourself 0 points.

INTERVIEWER'S QUESTION

[34] "Can you give an example of a time when you were able to convince others to change things your way?"

Select the strongest answer.

[A] My current boss is not very receptive to new ideas. I was able to sell her on one of my ideas when I showed her a marketing plan that I worked on to change some of the channels we were using for distribution. Behind the scenes, I put together a lot of data and analysis that included details, facts, and figures. That extra effort really paid off when I presented her with the idea. She is one of those people who need facts to make decisions. She trusted me a lot more after that.

[B] My boss would tell you that I am always selling him on ideas. I have at least one idea a week. Some work, and some don't. My success rate is about 75 percent positive. One of the frustrations that I have is getting through the approval stage. When you work for a large company, it sometimes can take weeks to get an idea through the mill. I am an action-oriented guy who wants to make things happen. Sometimes it takes so long to get an idea through the channels that it is less effective than it would be if I had been able to start on it when I first had the idea.

[C] Recently, I determined a need to market a product by using a different strategy. I met with my boss to convince her of my ideas, and she reluctantly gave me the go-ahead. I then met with the editorial, creative, and media departments. Working together, we planned media exposure, including TV, radio, print, newspaper, and interactive. We also put together a direct mail campaign. I calculated expenses and return on investment and presented it to my boss for approval. I really surprised her with the numbers and my estimated 30 percent return on investment. She gave a thumbs-up to proceed with the project. The result was absolutely great—not only did we have a dynamite success, but we saved more than $50,000 in costs.

ANSWERS

The Strongest Answer

[**C**] This is the strongest answer because of the example it gives of action on your part. The story parts are laid out: the situation, the action you took, the results. Showing a positive outcome makes for a good success story. There are times, however, when the outcome may not be positive for the company for reasons that are completely out of your control. When this is the case, keep the focus on your role in the project and the way you completed your task. Do not dwell on the company's problems. This is about you and the skills you have to offer. Talk about what you were responsible for and how your part of the deal worked even if there were no positive results. An example would be a project that was shelved after you did all the work to complete it. That was out of your control.

The Mediocre Answer

[**A**] This is not a bad answer, but it could be strengthened by more detail. Describing the analytic process and the types of facts and figures that you found and presented would have made the story stronger. The best part of this answer is your ability to understand that your boss has a style, which requires facts, and your ability to adapt your approach to meet her needs.

The Weakest Answer

[**B**] This answer is too general; it provides no facts. It starts out well with a 75 percent success rate—but then proceeds to complain about the company and the way it deals with the process. Since this may not be the way that this company handles such information, it is best to ask questions about the process first and then judge whether this culture is going to be different from the one you just left.

RATE YOURSELF

If you chose answer [**C**], give yourself 5 points.

If you chose answer [**A**], give yourself 3 points.

If you chose answer [**B**], give yourself 0 points.

INTERVIEWER'S QUESTION

[35] "Tell me about the last time you changed your personal style to adapt to a situation or another person's style. Describe the situation."

Select the strongest answer.

[A] Because I deal with a great many products and customers, I have to be very aware of the needs of the customer and act accordingly. For instance, I have some customers who are young and active and need clothes and shoes that correspond to their lifestyles. I make sure I know my customers and the needs of each individual. That has been a big part of my success in sales. I really like working with a broad range of people of all ages and stages.

[B] In my last position, I worked with a group of young people who were looking for clothes to wear on a camping trip. Rather than give them a pitch about what they "should" have, I asked them a few questions and then listened to what they had to say. I heard things that I wouldn't have thought of if I had jumped right in with my pitch. Based on what I heard, I put together a selection to present to them at our next meeting. They were pleasantly surprised that I had heard their requests.

[C] I consider the skill to adapt my style to the situation to be my major strength. I have the ability to change my personal style to adapt to the person I am working with. I take into consideration what the product is that I am trying to sell and who my customer is, and I adapt my style: the way I talk and what I say. This has been the most effective means for me to improve my communication skills and make more sales in the process.

ANSWERS

The Strongest Answer

[**B**] This answer provides the strongest example of a specific time when you adapted your style—and that was the question asked. The answer shows flexibility and the ability to know when to push and when to back off, which is an important trait in sales. It also demonstrates the ability to work with people of different ages and interests and do market research. Other skills shown are the ability to listen and the ability to follow through.

The Mediocre Answer

[**A**] This answer does not give a specific example, but it does give a "for instance" that, unfortunately, sounds generic. Although it talks about adaptability and customer service, it needs to show an actual example to be a stronger answer. *Show*—don't tell.

The Weakest Answer

[**C**] This is the weakest answer because it speaks in generalities. Like answer [**A**], it talks about adaptability, but it provides no concrete evidence that you have done what you say you can do. This would be a much stronger answer if you related a story about a time when you adapted your style.

RATE YOURSELF

If you chose answer [**B**], give yourself 5 points.

If you chose answer [**A**], give yourself 3 points.

If you chose answer [**C**], give yourself 0 points.

INTERVIEWER'S QUESTION

[36] "Give me an example of a time when you did more than the job required."

Select the strongest answer.

[A] I am a person who likes to stay busy. When my workload is down, I try to organize to be more efficient. As an example, while I was processing claims one day. I had the idea that the salespeople could enter claims online and shorten the entire process. I knew there was a better way of doing things, and so I put in some extra time designing a system that could be used as a prototype. I showed it to my boss, and she thought it was a great idea and design. In fact, she showed her boss. It eventually was incorporated into the company's process. I received a nice bonus for taking the initiative.

[B] I have a problem getting specific about this because going above and beyond is something I do all the time. I always get excellent performance appraisals and do the job as required. I try to help people whenever they have a problem. I feel people are very important to our business, and I am very responsive to customers' problems. I am a very dedicated support person who can be depended on to do the job and give it my full attention.

[C] I am a person who plans ahead, and I always have a good handle on the workload. Because I am extremely organized, I am never late and meet all my deadlines. I pride myself on my dependability. I always plan ahead, using reminders to myself. I put in whatever time is required. My boss would tell you that I am very efficient and have a great attitude about getting my work done and doing whatever it takes.

TIP By writing stories about your successes before the interview, you will be prepared to answer a number of questions and show that you have performed similar work successfully in the past. Your stories about your experiences are sometimes interchangeable and can be used to answer more than one question.

ANSWERS

The Strongest Answer

[**A**] This is the strongest answer because it gives an example of a time when you took the initiative and went beyond what the job required. The story has a beginning—the problem; it has a middle—the action you took; and it has a positive ending. In this answer, you show a very proactive approach to thinking of solutions to problems. This answer also could be used if you were asked about a time when you thought of a solution to a problem.

The Mediocre Answer

[**B**] This answer lacks a specific example. The ingredients for a good success story are there, but there is a need for detail. If you gave an example of a time when you went out of your way to help a customer with a problem, it would be a more relevant answer. Start with the specific problem, then describe the action you took, and end with how it turned out.

The Weakest Answer

[**C**] This is a weak answer because it is vague. It lists a lot of good skills but lacks examples of times when those skills were used. There is no story—no statement of the problem or situation and no action on your part. The strongest part of this answer is the indirect quote from your boss. It always works well to have a "third party" endorse your work.

RATE YOURSELF

If you chose answer [**A**], give yourself 5 points.

If you chose answer [**B**], give yourself 3 points.

If you chose answer [**C**], give yourself 0 points.

INTERVIEWER'S QUESTION

[37] "Give me an example of a time when you had to sacrifice quality to meet a deadline."

Select the strongest answer.

[A] I can't think of a time when I ever missed a deadline. Deadlines are really important in our business. In fact, I would go so far as to say that my job was completely deadline driven. There have been a few times when I had to plan my day to make sure that I did not miss deadlines. This usually meant long weeks with weekends and late nights. But I have always come through with a quality product. I recently was given an award for my record of keeping the customer satisfied by delivering the product on time.

[B] This happened recently. The company had a tight deadline, but because of circumstances beyond control, I knew that we could not make the delivery date and give a quality product. I did a quick analysis and determined that the only way I could meet the deadline would be to send the product without testing. I called the customer and explained the situation. I gave the customer a couple of alternatives with a recommendation to delay the shipping date to allow for proper testing. By offering options, I was able to get the customer to agree to extend the deadline. In the end, the product was shipped within three days. The customer later thanked me for my judgment in the matter.

[C] Deadlines don't move; my workday does. When I have a deadline that looks tight, I have to work harder. I often have to work nights, sometimes as late as midnight, and sometimes on weekends. Quality may get sacrificed from time to time, but we always meet the deadlines. I don't think there have ever been any circumstances where the customer complained about the delivery of the product. This is actually what I find most challenging about the job.

ANSWERS

The Strongest Answer

[**B**] This is the strongest answer. The deadline was not met, but the process for handling the problem makes this answer strong. The answer shows the use of judgment, problem-solving skills, negotiating skills, initiative, and communication skills. One of the reasons this is the best answer is that it makes it clear what the problem was, what your role was, and how it turned out. This is a good example of a complete story.

The Mediocre Answer

[**C**] This answer isn't bad, but an interviewer might wonder why you need to work such long hours. Is it because you are short-staffed or constantly behind in your workload? This answer also indicates a focus on deadlines only, with little regard for quality. Each job and company will have a different need for quality versus quantity. Depending on the position and the job, make sure that you answer with the focus where it belongs: working smarter—not longer.

The Weakest Answer

[**A**] This answer is weak because it does not give a specific example and it is focused on deadlines, not quality. In certain jobs where deadlines drive the business, this answer may be appropriate. However, in this case the question asked is about quality. The redeeming part of this answer is the mention of the award for delivering the product on time. One common problem in telling your story is not having a good ending to the story. Any time you can answer with a positive kudo or comment, it makes it a stronger story.

RATE YOURSELF

If you chose answer [**B**], give yourself 5 points.

If you chose answer [**C**], give yourself 3 points.

If you chose answer [**A**], give yourself 0 points.

INTERVIEWER'S QUESTION

[38] "What has been the most difficult training course or class you've ever taken?"

Select the strongest answer.

[A] That was while I was getting my BA degree. I was carrying a full load of credits and working a 30-hour week. I had a geology class that was the most difficult class I ever took. The way I survived was to plan the projects and study times, and I would stick to the plan no matter what. Because that class was the most difficult, I made sure that it was my main focus that semester. Focus was the key to surviving that course.

[B] I can't think of one course that was more difficult than the others. I have taken a lot of training courses since I graduated from college. Because I pick up things easily and quickly, I move right along. The classes and courses I have enjoyed the most have been about finance and investing. I have a good mind for numbers and theory, and that has helped me in my previous positions. I intend to keep taking classes as a way to develop new techniques.

[C] I've taken a lot of training courses in my career. Some of them have had to do with business, some with personal growth, and some with technology. I enjoy a broad coverage of subjects. I'm a strong believer in continual training. I guess the most difficult programs have been in the area of technology, which probably is my weakest area.

ANSWERS

The Strongest Answer

[**A**] This is the strongest answer because it is the most specific. Even though it is not about business, it gives a good example of how you focused your efforts to get through a tough situation. It is desirable to give a business answer as your first choice, but if you can't think of a situation that answers the question, give an answer that is as closely related to the question as possible. This is especially true for new grads or reentry persons. This answer indicates your ability to be organized and to plan as well as defining your tenacity. The skills demonstrated are the important aspect of this example.

The Mediocre Answer

[**C**] This answer is not wrong; it is just not as strong an answer as [**A**]. On the positive side, it does include the various kinds of training you've taken. In answer to this particular question, it would sound stronger if you focused on a specific course that challenged you the most. You say that the technology classes were the most difficult but don't give any of the specifics that would add depth to your answer. Also, you mention your weakness—not a good idea unless you are asked for that information.

The Weakest Answer

[**B**] This is the weakest answer because it does not answer the question and is very general. It has some merit because it speaks about your ability to learn quickly and pick up information easily. It also demonstrates an ethic of continual growth through learning, which is positive. But most important, the question was not answered with a specific example.

RATE YOURSELF

If you chose answer [**A**], give yourself 5 points.

If you chose answer [**C**], give yourself 3 points.

If you chose answer [**B**], give yourself 0 points.

INTERVIEWER'S QUESTION

[39] "Can you give me an example of a time when you were working on a project that required sustained and persistent effort?"

Select the strongest answer.

[A] I have handled all assignments with the same amount of effort. I do whatever it takes to get the job done. If I haven't been able to get my job done during the day, I will stay late to complete whatever it is that didn't get accomplished. I pride myself on getting the job done whatever it takes.

[B] The assignment that comes to mind is when I had a deadline to meet that would take three days to complete and I only had two days. What I did was to prioritize and delegate to other team members what I could. After that, I worked steadily by blocking off hours to work on nothing but the project. At the same time, I still had to get my regular work done. I put in a lot of extra hours, but for the most part, planning and prioritizing ahead made a huge difference, and I got the job done on time.

[C] I think the most sustained and persistent effort that I ever made was when I established a database for my last company. It was tedious work, and I had to work nonstop or I would lose the momentum of getting the task done. I am pretty good at concentrating when I have to. I got through the project and did a good job, but I was glad to be over with that tedious task.

ANSWERS

The Strongest Answer

[**B**] This is the strongest answer for several reasons. First, it shows that you listened to the question and answered what was asked: "Can you give me an example of a time when you were working on a project . . . ?" Your response also shows key qualities of planning, teamwork, and prioritizing. And you display an attitude of being willing to do whatever it takes to get the job done, as well as the ability to do it in a smart manner.

The Mediocre Answer

[**A**] Although the response doesn't really answer the question specifically, this is an OK answer because you share good information and the answer has the right energy behind it. The statement "I do whatever it takes to get the job done" doesn't cover a specific example of the behavior. If you cannot give a specific example, perhaps the words are empty and claim something that may not be quite true.

The Weakest Answer

[**C**] This answer is weak for several reasons. First, it shows that you lack confidence through the use of words such as "pretty good." You're either good or not good. Second, it has the tone of someone who had to make a real effort to get through a tedious task. Finally, depending on the job you are interviewing for, the interviewer might wonder whether you will burn out from the types of tasks you will need to perform in this position.

RATE YOURSELF

If you chose answer [**B**], give yourself 5 points.

If you chose answer [**A**], give yourself 3 points.

If you chose answer [**C**], give yourself 0 points.

INTERVIEWER'S QUESTION

[40] "Tell me about a time when you motivated a coworker or subordinate."

Select the strongest answer.

[A] I had a dotted-line responsibility for the support staff in my department. One of the women was really struggling with her workload. I talked to her and found out she was having problems at home and hadn't been able to attend some training classes. She was trying to pick up the information on her own. She agreed to work with me during her lunch hour or any time she could spare. I laid out a plan for her to follow and coached her on sections that needed explanation. She was a quick learner and came up to speed in less than three weeks. She was very grateful for my extra attention, and I was pleased with her performance improvement.

[B] My coaching skills are one of my strengths. I have coached several people inside and outside my department. Employees know that they can come to me for answers, and as a result, they seek me out. One of my basic rules when helping people is that they have to have tried to work their problems out on their own first. I can tell when someone is frustrated beyond the point of self-help and will try to work with him or her at that point. I don't believe in holding someone's hand, but I will help if an honest attempt has been made.

[C] I recently helped a coworker who was having real problems with the new system for tracking calls. She had missed some of the training sessions and was running behind with the new procedures. We were all so used to the old system that we could do it in a robotic state. But this new system was really complicated. The company put us through four weeks of training to learn the system, and even though I attended all the sessions, I had to put in extra effort to learn the details. She and I worked together, and she improved very quickly.

ANSWERS

The Strongest Answer

[**A**] This is the strongest answer because it provides a clear example of not only developing someone but going the extra mile to do so. This story is clear, with an explanation of the situation, a plan for carrying out the action, and an outcome. This is also an example of a story that would work if you were asked, "Tell me about a time when you went above and beyond what the job called for."

The Mediocre Answer

[**C**] This is not as strong an answer as [**A**] because it spends too much time explaining the problem and does not provide enough detail on the action or solution. There is very little evidence of what you did to help your coworker. This is a very common problem in relating behavioral stories. Spending more time on the action of the story (at least 60 percent) than on the problem or the result is crucial. Compare answers [**A**] and [**C**] to see the difference between a well-told story and one that is not specific and lacks a beginning, a middle, and an end.

The Weakest Answer

[**B**] This answer is not focused on developing or helping anyone in particular. While it has all the pieces of a good story, it mostly gives a lot of details about your philosophy of teaching or coaching; in the end, it provides little evidence that you actually have helped an individual. The interviewer does not have a clear picture of a time when you helped develop someone's skills by motivating the person.

RATE YOURSELF

If you chose answer [**A**], give yourself 5 points.

If you chose answer [**C**], give yourself 3 points.

If you chose answer [**B**], give yourself 0 points.

INTERVIEWER'S QUESTION

[41] "Give an example of a time when you were able to communicate with another person even when that individual may not have liked you personally (or vice versa)."

Select the strongest answer.

[A] I had a conflict with my manager—Jim—who was very upset with me. The problem began at the end of a workday. At that time, I had asked a coworker, Mary, if she needed any help and she told me no, and so I finished my work for that day and went home. The next day, Mary told Jim that I left her by herself and did not attempt to help with her workload. When I came into work that morning, Jim was standing at my desk and started yelling at me about the situation. I told him to calm down so we could talk about the matter. He refused to calm down and was berating me for taking advantage of my coworker because she is a woman. I calmly told him that there was a misunderstanding and that I wanted to explain my side of the story. I was able to get Jim into a conference room and talked to him at length. As a result, the situation was resolved; however, because of the situation, Jim would not speak to me unless it was work related. He later apologized for his behavior and said he had been going through some personal issues.

[B] I don't have conflicts with coworkers. I try to get along with everyone. Even if someone is annoying, I just ignore the situation. I think anyone I work with would tell you that I am a very nice person and a good coworker.

[C] There was a time when I had a conflict with someone at work. It was about a work issue. We basically just had a difference of opinion and had to work through some areas of responsibility. She was the type of person who made life miserable for others. She was responsible for at least two of our other employees leaving. She would never get caught by management because she was a very dishonest person and didn't tell the truth when conflicts were reported. She eventually left the firm, and I never saw her again.

ANSWERS

The Strongest Answer

[**A**] This is the strongest answer, not because it is the most lengthy but because it has the correct makeup of a good story. It describes in detail that there was a communication problem and that you were able to stay calm and handle the situation. A good story will be about two minutes long with the emphasis on the "action"—what steps were taken to resolve the issue.

The Mediocre Answer

[**C**] This is not a strong answer because you talk more about another person than you do about yourself. The question asked for an example of "a time when you were able to communicate with another person"; this answer is not an example of communication. When you talk in a negative tone about coworkers, that could be an indicator of the way you get along with others in the workplace. The interviewer is judging you on the examples of your past behavior as an indicator of how you will act in the job you are applying for.

The Weakest Answer

[**B**] This answer is clearly the weakest answer anyone can give to a behavioral question. The question distinctly asked for an example of "a time when . . ." This answer is more about your thoughts about communication with others. It also indicates a rather passive way of handling problems or conflict.

RATE YOURSELF

If you chose answer [**A**], give yourself 5 points.

If you chose answer [**C**], give yourself 3 points.

If you chose answer [**B**], give yourself 0 points.

INTERVIEWER'S QUESTION

[42] "Describe a time when you had to make an unpopular decision."

Select the strongest answer.

[A] In my analyst job, I worked with a team whose task was to target productivity studies. We had to explore all avenues and options in solving problems and making recommendations. This sometimes included laying people off. We labored over our decisions so that we would be fair and objective. We then had to present our findings to upper management and stand by our decisions even though they sometimes were challenged. Most of our recommendations were accepted and resulted in a decreased labor cost of 30 percent by laying off personnel.

[B] I thoroughly explore all avenues in targeting productivity studies. Only as a last resort would I recommend laying people off, which probably is considered the most unpopular decision a manager can make. Sometimes I make recommendations for procedural changes that can be unpopular with employees. Change often is viewed negatively. The more popular recommendations that I have made include streamlining procedures and computerizing processes, which saved money and time.

[C] Decisions affecting people's lives are the most difficult. In my last job, I conducted a productivity study that determined that some jobs were redundant. I was in charge of a committee that would decide who would be laid off. As the team's leader, I was responsible for putting together the basic criteria for the decision. I did an analysis of the positions and people, their seniority, their salaries, and their job content. The group had to make decisions on the basis of the standards I set up. It went smoothly and resulted in a 30 percent cost saving, but it didn't make the decisions any easier or popular.

TIP Most interviewers will remember only one or two points from your story. Make sure that your story is focused and that it answers the question asked. When you stray from the original example, you confuse the interviewer.

ANSWERS

The Strongest Answer

[**C**] This is the strongest answer because it gives a detailed picture of your actions in putting together the criteria to make a strong decision; this shows the interviewer that you are willing to take on a task even though it may not be popular with the rest of the employees. This is a good example of your leadership and preparedness. It is also a strong answer because it is quantified. Whenever possible, quantify, or give a number, to establish the scope of the situation.

The Mediocre Answer

[**A**] This answer is not as strong as answer [**C**] because there is no indication of your role in this example. Even when you are part of a team, you need to convey what you did as a team member. When you talk about the situation, be sure to include yourself and your role in the project as part of the story. The use of the pronouns we and I are important to your story—making sure that your role is defined.

The Weakest Answer

[**B**] This answer is the weakest because it lacks focus and, of course, does not answer the question asked. It starts out well, takes a turn down a different road, and ends up with your philosophy and some disjointed comments. The question clearly asked for a specific time when you made an "unpopular decision." Thinking about the question and focusing on one or two points will make the answer more succinct. All stories must have a beginning, a middle, and an end to be successful.

RATE YOURSELF

If you chose answer [**C**], give yourself 5 points.

If you chose answer [**A**], give yourself 3 points.

If you chose answer [**B**], give yourself 0 points.

INTERVIEWER'S QUESTION

[43] "Tell me about the most creative project you've worked on."

Select the strongest answer.

[A] I created a multimedia lecture series that was based on the history of film by incorporating film footage from various movies and TV shows through the years to support me with some of the new things that I was attempting. I came up with an idea for presenting the award-winning films through the last 50 years of film and showing how computerization could have changed the effect. Then I used the techniques used today to demonstrate how far film has advanced. The crew I worked with gave me great praise for my original way of presenting the idea, using the latest technology available.

[B] I try to put a new spin on all my projects instead of repeating the same old stuff. I did a project recently on the history of film that turned out better than expected. My secret to being creative is to look at what's been done before and then try something completely new. I am known for my originality and creativity among my peers and others I have worked with. I have worked nationally and internationally and have a broad view of what it takes to be creative in this business.

[C] In my business, it is especially important to think outside the box. Every project I work on presents a new challenge. Whether I'm working with private collections or museum displays or working on live-action short films, I am excited by the challenge of the medium. I am known for my work with film and have been praised by all concerned, including my camera crews.

ANSWERS

The Strongest Answer

[**A**] This answer provides a clear example of what you did and what methods you used to accomplish a successful outcome. This is also a good example of letting the interviewer know that you have done this type of work before and can do it again. Mentioning that the crew thought highly of your work is a good way to provide an endorsement from people who worked with you.

The Mediocre Answer

[**B**] This answer isn't as strong as [**A**] because it is not as clear and specific. It touches on a particular project but doesn't provide the details that will let the interviewer know the skills you used or your method of working. This answer has some good material but needs more detail to show a good picture of you through a balanced story format.

The Weakest Answer

[**C**] This answer fails to focus on creativity. It shows a definite interest in film and an enthusiasm for different media, but it does not mention any projects you worked on that would tell the interviewer specifically how you carried out your creative work. Even the endorsement given is too general to be of much significance.

RATE YOURSELF

If you chose answer [**A**], give yourself 5 points.

If you chose answer [**B**], give yourself 3 points.

If you chose answer [**C**], give yourself 0 points.

INTERVIEWER'S QUESTION

[44] "You say you have good customer service skills. Tell me about a time when you used good customer service skills in your job."

Select the strongest answer.

[A] Good customer service is the name of the game, and I believe that the internal customers and the external customers are equally important. The first rule of good customer service is that you have to take care of your customer or your account will take its business elsewhere. I try to make the customer right every time, within reason. We have to live by our corporate rules, and even if they are unreasonable, we do our best to hold to company policy. I try to work as a liaison between corporate and the sales reps, smoothing out problems.

[B] In my current job, I resolved a customer problem that involved one of our sales reps and another company. I worked as a liaison between our rep and the corporate office. The rep was very upset because we weren't standing behind our warranty on a product he sold to that company. The first thing I did was to pull the appropriate paperwork, and then I made a recommendation to our corporate office. I laid out the facts, and we had a bit of a negotiation. In the end, everything turned out well for the rep and the customer. The rep couldn't thank me enough. He said that I saved the account.

[C] In my 10 years working with customers, I have had numerous compliments on my service skills from my customers and reps. I often work directly with customers, and sometimes I work as a liaison between our sales reps and corporate. Because I am a person who is very organized and pays attention to details, I am able to pull together the facts and present the case in a more organized manner. Not only does this process empower me to do what I can do to help, but it also gives my reps a feeling that someone is on their side.

> **Tip** When you are in an interview, your answers will be much longer and more detailed—especially in the action portion. A good length for an answer is about two minutes or so. You want to give as much detail as possible, but you also want to keep the interviewer's attention.

ANSWERS

The Strongest Answer

[**B**] This is the strongest answer because it answers the question with a good example of your work as a liaison between the sales reps (your customer) and corporate and the way you used a number of good customer service skills. Some of the skills demonstrated are research, organization, and negotiation skills. It also provides a good example of taking the initiative and recommending a solution rather than asking for advice and putting the problem on corporate.

The Mediocre Answer

[**C**] This is not a bad answer; it just is not specific enough. The answer speaks about skills but does not give an example. The interviewer asks for proof or backup of the claim that you have good customer service skills. Any time you mention a skill on your résumé or during an interview, the interviewer may ask you to prove it with an example.

The Weakest Answer

[**A**] This answer is the weakest one because it preaches to the interviewer. The interviewer already knows that customer service is important and that if people cannot provide good customer service, the company will lose business. Another negative aspect of this answer is that it complains about corporate policy and the need to follow it in spite of its being unreasonable. This is not a good tone to take in an interview because it could indicate that you are someone who is passive and does the work but really does not believe in what the company stands for. There are many companies to choose from; it is best to determine which company's business philosophy is in line with yours as much as possible. An example of a bad match is an environmentally concerned person going to work for a pesticide company.

RATE YOURSELF

If you chose answer [**B**], give yourself 5 points.

If you chose answer [**C**], give yourself 3 points.

If you chose answer [**A**], give yourself 0 points.

INTERVIEWER'S QUESTION

[45] "Tell me about a time when your communication skills made a difference."

Select the strongest answer.

[A] My skills are strong in written and oral communications. I write a great deal of the curriculum for teaching programs. I've worked with great teams and focused on the invaluable role of art as a source of cultural enrichment in our everyday lives. I have written interactive exercises and developed creative test models that are used as standards in the schools where I have worked. Communication with the teams I have worked with has made a huge difference in the success of my projects. I couldn't have done it without their cooperation and communication.

[B] I have over five years of experience developing and delivering programs for schools. I develop, organize, and conduct educational tours to Europe, focusing on relaying the role of art and history as cultural enrichment in our everyday lives. I coauthored and helped produce a series of art videos that are used in educational institutions throughout the United States. I am known for my passionate delivery and presentation of materials that have been viewed as uninteresting when presented by others. It's the way you present the information that makes the difference.

[C] One project I worked on involved developing the curriculum for a program dealing with cultural similarities in everyday life. The challenge was to communicate with my team members and get them as excited about their roles in the project as I was about mine. I talked to them individually, drawing out the particular interests they had. I used this information to assign responsibilities, enabling me to bring about extremely positive results through a team effort. The feedback from the individual members of the team was that they all felt they had made a contribution in their own special way. It was worth the extra effort taken to listen and obtain their input.

ANSWERS

The Strongest Answer

[**C**] This is the strongest answer because of the specific example and focus on the way you used communication skills to work with individuals, listening and implementing the ideas heard. Because good communication skills involve listening and writing as well as speaking, you have demonstrated a broad use of your skills. This is an answer that also shows strong leadership skills as well as the ability to appreciate the differences people bring to a situation.

The Mediocre Answer

[**A**] This answer has all the makings of a good story, but it is not specific. It just needs to be rearranged to focus on the communication issues and address the question. If you compare this example with [**C**], the strongest answer, you can see how the same information is given, but with more emphasis placed on communication with the team that brought about successful results.

The Weakest Answer

[**B**] This answer speaks about your experiences as they are written on your résumé, not as a relevant example of your experience. A specific example of any one of the skills you mentioned would be stronger than reiterating your résumé content. The last of this answer could be developed as an example of your presentation to a group and the feedback you obtained about your passionate delivery.

RATE YOURSELF

If you chose answer [**C**], give yourself 5 points.

If you chose answer [**A**], give yourself 3 points.

If you chose answer [**B**], give yourself 0 points.

INTERVIEWER'S QUESTION

[46] "Describe an assignment that required you to take care of the greatest number of details."

Select the strongest answer.

[A] You can't do the type of work I do and not pay strong attention to details. I am known for being very accurate. In fact, my team members bring me their work to check for accuracy. I have a natural eye for detail. I have always been great at proofreading and picking up errors. I have worked on statements with thousands of figures, and I have just kept at it until I have all the entries correct. One time it took me a week of tedious checking of facts and numbers, but in the end I had a quality product. It would bother me a lot if my work went out with errors.

[B] I recently worked on a project that included lots of details. The way I work is to set up spreadsheets and track the details and my progress. By making sure that all the entries are correct and that I meet my deadline, I have had great success with projects. My last project made a big difference in the efficiency of customer repair orders. I pride myself on checking and rechecking details whenever I am working on a project. Sometimes I have my teammates check my work to make sure that I haven't made any mistakes. On my performance appraisals, my boss always mentions what great attention to detail I have.

[C] In one of my earlier jobs, I set up an in-house tracking system for customer repair units. I organized all the data collected to-date and entered the times the order was taken against the time elapsed before the repair was complete. It was important to assure accuracy in the initial setup of this system, and so I hand-sorted and entered all the information myself and had a team member check my entries. We ran a trial run to assure that everything was working, and the results were flawless. This project reduced the turnaround time on customer orders by 50 percent. I was given a lot of praise for my precise work, and I also received a nice bonus.

ANSWERS

The Strongest Answer

[**C**] This is the strongest answer because of the specific detail given. There is a firm indication of a need to be accurate but not compulsive. The answer also shows other qualities, such as being organized and collaborating with other team members. By quantifying the savings made to the company and the rewards given, you make a stronger impact. If you did it before, you can do it again.

The Mediocre Answer

[**B**] This answer is not as strong as [**A**] because it places the emphasis of the story in the wrong place and buries the most important information. It starts out by being specific and then lapses into general information. By saying "My last project made a big difference in the efficiency of customer repair orders," you have minimized the effect of the project. Answer [**C**] states that the project reduced the turnaround time by 50 percent, which is far more specific and impressive.

The Weakest Answer

[**A**] This is the weakest answer because it lacks specific details and also because it may be seen as somewhat compulsive. By giving a specific example of a time when you had a project that involved many details you took care of, you would soften the impact of always having to be accurate. Any good trait that is taken to extreme becomes a negative.

RATE YOURSELF

If you chose answer [**C**], give yourself 5 points.

If you chose answer [**B**], give yourself 3 points.

If you chose answer [**A**], give yourself 0 points.

INTERVIEWER'S QUESTION

[47] "Describe a time when you used good judgment and logic in solving a problem."

Select the strongest answer.

[A] I have always been told that my problem-solving skills and my judgment and logic are superior. As early as high school and then into college, I have been praised for my rational approach to solving problems. I always look at as much available information as I can to determine what the problems or issues are. I then take a look at past behavior. I believe that history is the best way to judge the future. I have been praised for my logical thinking and my ability to analyze information.

[B] Some people are born with the ability to figure things out logically, and I am one of those people. It just comes naturally to me. I have always been extremely good at math and took some engineering classes in college. I have excelled in any endeavors I have tried by using logic and analysis. I think I also have good common sense when it comes to making judgments. I try not to overthink problems—but do a thorough job of research to determine the value and the risk of taking actions.

[C] One of my jobs was to evaluate companies and investment options. Sometimes I was required to look into an industry or country that I knew nothing about. This was the case when one day my boss asked me to come up with some investment ideas for another country. Since I knew very little about the country, let alone possible investments, the first thing I did was a lot of reading. I researched everything from social and political issues, to successful industries, to laws and the way foreign investments were treated. Next, I spoke to a former classmate who lived in the country and was working there for a local company. Once I had a good overview of the country and its economy, I summarized my findings in a one-page report for my boss. The whole assignment took me a little over a week to complete. I have become skilled at researching, evaluating, and efficiently summarizing my findings. My boss praised my successful analysis.

ANSWERS

The Strongest Answer

[**C**] This is a good example of a complete story, even though the answer is a somewhat shortened version of one you would actually give in an interview. It provides an effective example of a particular time when research and planning were important to the end result. Because of limited space here, many of the details have been left out, but during an interview, you would give more information and offer many more details to give a strong example of how you use resources—research, reading, networking—to come to your conclusion. By summarizing your findings in a one-page report, you are demonstrating an ability to break data down into reasonable and usable portions.

The Mediocre Answer

[**A**] This answer only fails because it is not specific. There is good information to show what your approach to solving problems is. It is clear that you know how to solve a problem using past behavior or results, but to answer the question asked—in this case a behavioral question asking for an example—you must give a specific instance. Just as you look at past behavior for your research, so is the interviewer using past behavior to judge your future performance as an employee.

The Weakest Answer

[**B**] This answer doesn't come close to answering the question or giving any type of specific example. It's more like a "brag session" about all the good things that you can do. There are some areas of concern—for example, "I try not to overthink"—that might cause an interviewer to probe further into possible behavior patterns.

RATE YOURSELF

If you chose answer [**C**], give yourself 5 points.

If you chose answer [**A**], give yourself 3 points.

If you chose answer [**B**], give yourself 0 points.

INTERVIEWER'S QUESTION

[48] "Describe a time that required you to do a number of things at the same time, and explain how you chose what got top priority."

Select the strongest answer.

[A] This is pretty much my day-to-day work routine—juggling many projects at one time. There are days when I have as many as 20 clients, and I'm sometimes trying to take calls and solve problems for 20 more people. I have a very high customer satisfaction rating. One thing I've learned to do is to prioritize my projects according to deadlines that need to be met. I am pretty efficient at meeting deadlines. It sometimes takes some negotiation on my part, but I really like staying with a good challenge and getting things done.

[B] The first thing that I do when I have a deadline is to make up a spreadsheet and put in all my information regarding dates and deadlines. I also make sure that I have an ongoing list of things that need to be accomplished. And I always put together a list of the "players" involved and their contact information. This becomes my bible of resources and people that will help me to meet deadlines or solve problems. This program really works because everyone has access to the database so that we can track each team member's progress. I have become my department's hero as a result of everyone seeing how well it works.

[C] This happened at my last company when my manager and one support person left at the same time for different reasons. I was thrust into a position to keep things running smoothly. One of the things I had to do was to make sure that all obligations were satisfied and deadlines were met. What I did to decide which projects were more important than others was to ask each project manager some key questions. I then took their answers and used them to determine important deadlines. Next I created a program using my Outlook Calendar to track and remind those involved that a deadline was looming. My program was considered to be very successful, and I received many compliments and kudos from both staff and management.

ANSWERS

The Strongest Answer

[**C**] This is the strongest and most specific answer regarding your ability to prioritize and plan. If this question were to be asked in your interview, your answer would be longer with more detail. The more specific and detailed the answer is to a behavioral question, the stronger the story.

The Mediocre Answer

[**B**] Although the right words are there, this answer is too general and lacks the specifics of your work. It is very tempting to use your method of operation and to describe what you do in situations like this. But remember the interviewer asking behavioral questions wants specific examples. To be a stronger answer, this would need to start with "I remember one incident in particular . . ." The question asks for "a" time, not what you do day by day.

The Weakest Answer

[**A**] The problem with this answer is that it is way too general. It has the right content but needs to be rearranged in order to answer this question. Be sure to pick a particular time when you juggled projects and gave high customer service satisfaction. By giving an example, the interviewer gets a stronger idea of what your pattern of behavior will be in this job.

RATE YOURSELF

If you chose answer [**C**], give yourself 5 points.

If you chose answer [**B**], give yourself 3 points.

If you chose answer [**A**], give yourself 0 points.

INTERVIEWER'S QUESTION

[49] "Tell me about a time when you were self-motivated to achieve and succeed."

Select the strongest answer.

[A] I am driven by my own success. When I am performing well, I am driven to do better. We write marketing plans and goals each quarter, and I live by those plans, attempting to make as many calls and sales as I have projected. If I fall behind in my calls, I have to readjust my plan to make up for the slack, and this drives me even harder. It works well for me. I feel good about succeeding and am driven to go on as long as I continue to get results and am rewarded for my efforts.

[B] Competition is usually a great driver for me. The more incentive that is offered to me by the company, the more I am driven toward results. I can motivate myself by setting quotas to make a certain amount of calls every day, but it helps if there is a reward along the lines of a bonus or percentage of sales to drive me harder. I work hard and do whatever it takes to maintain my accounts. I believe the secret to good sales is persistence and follow-up. I have built a reputation for being there for my customers.

[C] I needed to stimulate interest with my customers and decided to hold a competition. I personally had accumulated a ton of frequent-flier miles and came up with the idea of offering an incentive for customers to let me introduce the new product. The deal was that every customer who let me demonstrate the product was entered into a drawing for a trip to Hawaii. I sent out letters and e-mails explaining the contest and had great results. I knew that once I was able to demonstrate the product, I could sell it. I came in tops in my division.

ANSWERS

The Strongest Answer

[**C**] This is the strongest answer because it shows original thinking and presents a solid example of a time when you were driven to succeed. This answer can be used to answer other questions such as "Tell me about a time when you came up with a creative strategy" or "Tell me about a time when you were able to think outside the box."

The Mediocre Answer

[**A**] This answer talks about being driven and motivated but does not give a specific example to make it stronger. Self-motivation is a good quality to use in your stories, but anyone can say he or she is self-motivated. When you give an example of an actual time when you were driven, as done in answer [**C**], it has a stronger impact.

The Weakest Answer

[**B**] This is a weak answer that dwells on what kind of incentive the company can give you to motivate and drive you rather than the way you drive yourself. The interview should focus on what you can do for the company, not on what the company can do for you.

RATE YOURSELF

If you chose answer [**C**], give yourself 5 points.

If you chose answer [**A**], give yourself 3 points.

If you chose answer [**B**], give yourself 0 points.

INTERVIEWER'S QUESTION

[50] "Tell me about the most difficult sale you had to make. What did you do to get the sale?"

Select the strongest answer.

[A] The first thing I do in a difficult sales situation is talk to the decision maker. I recently talked with a man who had started the business himself and took pride in his product. I acknowledged his accomplishment and inquired what the next level of sales for his business would be. He told me he was expanding and adding a delivery service. Before I could tell him what I had to offer, I asked a lot more questions about his vision and listened carefully to what he said. I had to get his trust before he would share his plans. Taking time to ask questions and listen carefully has made a huge difference in my success. I was able to sell him a bigger ad than he originally planned to buy.

[B] This is the challenge of sales: selling to customers when they are not necessarily receptive to buying. I have been in this business almost 10 years, and the majority of my sales have been difficult. When you call a business, you can get the same old response of "not interested." What I do is develop a plan for myself to hit a certain amount of calls per day. By setting a goal for myself, I focus on the goal, not on the rejection. I've been at it long enough to know the techniques that can overcome objections and get me an appointment. Once I get the appointment, I know how to sell.

[C] The first thing I do when I am trying to sell a product, whether to individuals or to companies, is to find out what their needs are and what they will do with the product. I do this by listening to the needs of the customer and sometimes reading between the lines. I always reiterate what I heard through active listening. The customer responds well to my being able to "hear" his or her problem. Once I have established the need, I can begin to talk about my product as the solution to the problem. I have established great rapport with customers by using this technique.

ANSWERS

The Strongest Answer

[**A**] This is the strongest answer because it not only gives a specific answer but talks about your sales technique, providing a clear example of a successful sale. The example given shows a lot of patience and customer savvy on your part, recognizing that timing and trust are everything when you are selling someone a new product or idea.

The Mediocre Answer

[**C**] Although this answer has good content, it does not provide a specific example. This answer would get the point across if it included an application of the theory it outlines. Do you recognize the theory as being the way you should approach the job interview? Listen to "their" problem before you sell yourself as the solution to the problem. This is a basic sales technique, and it works well in an interview.

The Weakest Answer

[**B**] This is the weakest answer because it describes your basic selling philosophy rather than your method of operation. Instead of talking about a specific difficult sale, you are focusing on your techniques and how you go about preparing for a sale. You are saying that you can overcome objections but are not giving any concrete examples of your successes.

RATE YOURSELF

If you chose answer [**A**], give yourself 5 points.

If you chose answer [**C**], give yourself 3 points.

If you chose answer [**B**], give yourself 0 points.

Interview IQ Scorecard:
What's Your Interview IQ Score?

Insert your score for each question in the blank following it. Then calculate your total score for all 50 questions.

General Questions

1. "Tell me about yourself."_____

2. "Why did you leave (or why are you planning to leave) your last position?"_____

3. "Why do you want to work here?" _____

4. "What are your goals?" _____

5. "What are your strengths?"_____

6. "What is your greatest weakness?" _____

7. "When have you been most motivated?"_____

8. "How would your coworkers describe your personality?"

    _____

9. "Have you ever been fired?" _____

10. "I see you have been out of work for some time. Why has it taken you so long to find a job?" _____

11. "What experience do you have that qualifies you for this position?" _____

12. "How would your current or last boss describe your job performance?" _____

13. "What do you know about this company?"_____

14. "Have you ever had a deadline that you missed? Why did you miss it?" _____

15. "What can you do for us that the other candidates can't?"

    _____

16. "In what ways has your current or last job prepared you to take on more responsibility?"_____

17. "What do you value most in a team?" _____

18. "What are the most important things for you in any job or company?" _____

19. "How do you stay current and informed about industry trends and technology?" _____

20. "Do you work well under pressure?" _____

21. "If I asked your coworkers to say three positive things about you, what would they say?" _____

22. "How have you contributed to teamwork in your jobs?"

    _____

23. "If I remember only one thing about you, what should that be?" _____

24. "What are your salary expectations?" _____

25. "Do you have any questions?"_____

Behavioral Questions

26. "Tell me about the biggest project you've worked on from start to finish."_____

27. "Describe a time when you had to adapt to a new situation."

    _____

28. "Tell me about a time when you had to handle a stressful situation."_____

29. "Your résumé states that you're a hard worker. Can you give me an example of a time when you worked hard?" _____

30. "Tell me about a time when you had a disagreement or conflict with a boss or coworker." _____

31. "What was the most difficult problem you've handled? How did you deal with it?" _____

32. "Tell me about a time when you had to adapt quickly to a change." _____

33. "Can you give me an example of working in a fast-paced environment?" _____

34. "Can you give us an example of a time when you were able to convince others to change things your way?" _____

35. "Tell me about the last time you changed your personal style to adapt to a situation or another person's style. Describe the situation." _____

36. "Give me an example of a time when you did more than the job required." _____

37. "Give me an example of a time when you had to sacrifice quality to meet a deadline."_____

38. "What has been the most difficult training course or class you've ever taken?" _____

39. "Can you give me an example of a time when you were working on a project that required sustained and persistent effort?"

_____

40. "Tell me about a time when you motivated a coworker or subordinate." _____

41. "Give me an example of a time when you were able to communicate with another person even when that individual may not have liked you personally (or vice versa)." _____

42. "Describe a time when you had to make an unpopular decision." _____

43. "Tell me about the most creative project you've worked on."

_____

44. "You say you have good customer service skills. Tell me about a time when you used good customer service skills in your job." _____

45. "Tell me about a time when your communication skills made a difference." _____
46. "Describe an assignment that required you to take care of the greatest number of details." _____
47. "Describe a time when you used good judgment and logic in solving a problem." _____
48. Describe a time that required you to do a number of things at the same time, and explain how you chose what got top priority." _____
49. "Tell me about a time when you were self-motivated to achieve and succeed." _____
50. "Tell me about the most difficult sale you had to make. What did you do to get the sale?" _____

Total score _____

Rate Yourself: Score Evaluation

Evaluate your total points as follows:

Interview Ability Rating System

▶ *176 to 250 points: genius level.* If you've scored in this range, you've got the idea. Now use your technique to prepare your own stories.

▶ *100 to 175 points: above-average level.* The "story" format will enhance your answers and give you more success in the interview. Read Part 2 and then retake the test. You will be ready to prepare your own stories.

▶ *Below 100 points: average level.* It's OK to start out at this level. Preparation and practice will only improve your stories, your confidence, and your results. Read Part 2 and retake the test until you have achieved a higher score. Then write your own stories.

PART II

The Surefire Way
to Boost Your Score

Unlocking the Secrets to Successful Interviewing

Above all, the secret to success in any interview is preparation. Can you imagine making a presentation to a group of people without knowing what you were going to say? Probably not. But how do you prepare for an interview when you don't know what the topic will be? How can you know what the interviewer will ask you? There is no way to predict what you will be asked in an interview, but there are four steps that will help you deal with the questions that will be asked. Read on!

Step 1. Understanding Today's Interviewing Techniques

In this section, we will discuss behavioral questions (these are also called performance-based questions) and situational questions (traditional-type questions).

What Is Behavioral Interviewing?

This type of interviewing technique involves questions that seek to determine your behavior—in particular, your past behavior—as an indicator of your future success. In other words, the answers you give about your past experiences will be used to predict your future performance: if you did it before, you can do it again. This includes both positive and negative behavior.

A Brief History of Behavioral Interviewing

Before we discuss creating your own stories, let's start by examining the reason companies use behavioral interviewing techniques. In the 1970s, industrial psychologists developed a new way to predict whether a person would succeed in a job. On the basis of the principle that future performance can be predicted by examining past behavior, candidates were asked questions that requested proof, often in the form of examples, that they had done what they claimed to be able to do.

Research performed over the last three decades indicates that when only traditional interview questions are asked during an interview, up to 75 percent of the people hired do not meet the performance expectations after they start the job. Some candidates interview well, but when it comes to performance, they aren't who they claimed to be. According to an article titled "Improv at the Interview" in the February 3, 2003, issue of *BusinessWeek*, companies that have adopted behavioral interviewing techniques claim to make better hiring decisions and to have as much as five times more success with retention and performance than they were getting when they used the traditional interviewing style.

In today's job market, in which there are so many applicants to choose from, employers must make accurate hiring decisions and rely on more effective ways to screen candidates. Because of costly hiring mistakes, employers have become more cautious about hiring on the basis of "gut feelings." According to *BusinessWeek*, standard interviews have a 7 percent rate of accuracy in their predictions as opposed to situational interviewing. An interviewer uses behavioral interviewing techniques to draw out specific examples of a job candidate's past behavior to determine the candidate's ability to perform in similar circumstances. In other words, what past behavior can this person bring to this company? What successes will be repeated in this job? Will the skills and knowledge this person already possesses save the company time, money, or labor power?

As the interviewer finds out more about the way you act, your method of operation, and the way you handle situations, a profile or picture of you is formed from the answers and examples you give. This profile indicates quite a lot about your skill sets, attitude, and ability to cope in various situations.

If the interviewer asks a question that sounds like "Tell me about a time when" or "Can you give me an example?" you should immediately think "story."

When you hear a question that begins by asking for an example, you will know that the interviewer is seeking information about your past behavior. In other words, she or he is asking for a specific example of a time when you dealt with a similar experience. If you give a general answer or fabricate an answer to this type of question, not only will that response fail to answer the question, but it may backfire when the interviewer begins to probe for more information.

When you hear a behavioral question, it's your cue that the interviewer is looking for an example of one of your specific experiences. Your answer should relate an incident in which you were involved. Here's an example.

Interviewer's Question

"Tell me about a time when you started a new job and had to meet a group of people you'd never met before." (*Hint:* You know from the question that the interviewer is seeking to learn about a specific time when you began a new job and how you related to people.)

Answer

(Problem/Situation)
"When I started my last job, one of the challenges that I faced was getting to know a group of people who were not very happy that I got the job because an internal person was hoping to get the position. So you might say that I had a hostile greeting. I didn't let that bother me, as I had been in similar situations over the course of my career."

(Action)
"The first thing I did was take a couple of days to get to know who did what and identify some of the people who needed special 'handling.' My

boss was very helpful about filling me in and introducing me around the various departments. Because I had to interface with several of the most hostile persons as part of my responsibilities, I set up appointments to meet with those people individually.

I made sure that my calendar was clear so that I could focus on one person at a time with no interruptions. When we had a meeting, one of the first things I told the person was that I was a hands-on manager, and I quoted some of the things my last team had said about me. I'm known for my partnering. My previous team members called me Reliable Sam because they knew I would come through for them in the clutch. This approach seemed to soften their attitude.

I did a lot more listening than I did talking through the meetings and came away with a great deal of information and new confidence that I could work with this team.

I made some promises to them in regard to some additional resources I could provide, and I made sure that I made good on each promise."

(Result)
"In the end, I won over each member within the month. I think my success was due to my waiting and not rushing in before I saw the lay of the land. My boss was really impressed with my ability to win them over."

The interviewer has heard some valuable information about you through this specific example of your actions. Some of the skill sets you've revealed through this answer include problem-solving skills, communication skills, listening skills, analytical skills, leadership skills, initiative, resourcefulness, and the ability to influence others.

You've presented your role, in this example walking through the specific steps you took to solve the problem. The interviewer is beginning to hear that you have the experience you claimed on your résumé. Remember, anyone can say that he or she is a good problem solver, but not everyone can give a specific example of a time when he or she solved a problem by providing specific details and facts as proof.

You can see the advantage of telling your story to convey your behavior: the interviewer gets a more accurate picture of you and learns about your skills and abilities and the ways you used them in the past. Remember that even when you are not asked behavioral questions, you can still use your stories by saying to the interviewer, "Let me tell you about a time when I solved a similar problem for my last employer." In other words, give an example if appropriate, even when you are not asked for one.

Stories Demonstrating Your Skills

Your examples are best told through a story format. The more interesting and relevant your story is, the more the interviewer will want to hear further examples.

As we discussed above, a question that asks you to "tell me about a time" must address "a time" when you dealt with a situation. If you do not provide a specific example, you will fail to answer the question and will have missed an opportunity to relate what you have to bring to this job on the basis of your past successes.

Unless you have thought about this type of questioning ahead of time, you may find yourself caught off-guard and be unable to respond with the strongest answer on the spot. The challenge of answering these questions is to select the right story: the one that shows off your skills and abilities in the best possible manner. The problem is that you may have had many years of work experience and have solved lots of problems.

The interviewer is listening for specific examples from you and stories about the way you performed in a similar job or role. If you were a marketing professional and came up with an original idea for a new campaign, and if the campaign was successful and brought in new business, your story will have a great impact because the interviewer will be hopeful that you can repeat that success.

You may wonder about the following:

▶ *Which problem does this interviewer want to hear about?* Always relate the story to the job description or ad and target what the employer is looking for. If the employer wants a focus on customer service, prepare stories about the times when you had great success with the customers.

▶ *How much detail should I go into?* Detail is important as long as it is relevant. If the employer is looking for a problem solver and that is your particular talent, let the interviewer hear about the method you use to solve problems, such as analyzing, asking questions, using trial and error, or doing whatever makes you a successful problem solver.

▶ *What is this interviewer looking for?* The interviewer is looking for someone who can come in and do the work and solve the problems—someone who has had the right past experiences or knowledge and knows how to make good judgments and work hard. Let the interviewer know what you have to bring; this includes your transferable skills and personal traits.

Preparing your examples before the interview will give you a head start in being able to provide answers to behavioral questions. There is nothing worse than leaving an interview and regretting that you did not tell the interviewer about a time when you excelled. If you leave the interview and haven't given the interviewer a complete picture of "you," it will be a lost opportunity that you cannot go back and do over. Preparing your examples—or stories—before the interview is essential to your success. Preparation will make or break your chances of convincing the interviewer that you have had the experience needed for this job.

To prepare, think about your stories—and write them down—before the interview. Doing this preparation enables you to select the stories that prove your claim that you are experienced. It is also an opportunity to demonstrate your skills and abilities through examples of past successes. When you prepare ahead of the interview, you can select the stories that show your abilities in the best light. The following material discusses the elements of a strong story. Once you've mastered these elements, the rest of the book will teach you how to prepare your own stories.

The Elements of Your Story

A key precept for answering behavioral questions is this: *behavioral questions require a complete and specific example or story.* The interviewer will have a much easier job listening to and following your stories if they are laid out in a chronological, easy-to-follow sequence of events. The most successful stories include the following elements:

Beginning. What the problem was

Middle. What you did about the problem

End. How it turned out

Let's examine each of the story parts in the following example.

Interviewer's Question

"Tell about a time when you successfully solved a problem in your past experience."

> **Rule 1.** Listen to the clues in the question; they will tell you what your answer should focus on—in this case, a

specific time when you solved a problem. The first thing you must do is let the interviewer know what the problem was by defining the problem or situation in a way that is to the point.

Answer's Beginning

(Problem/Situation)

"I worked in the customer service department in my last company and was responsible for dealing with the escalated problem calls—basically people who were beyond complaining and were ready to cancel their orders. I was receiving lots of complaints from customers who were not able to get through to the customer service line to place their orders. The delay, or waiting period, sometimes was at least five minutes and sometimes longer."

Here the problem is conveyed in a clear and concise manner. You have set the stage. The interviewer now knows what the problem was and what your role was in the example you will be providing.

Rule 2. Include action steps in your answer to make it clear to the interviewer what you did about the problem. In other words, what skills did you use? What was your method of operation?

Answer's Middle

(Action)

"The first step I took was to find out why the problem existed. I interviewed the people who were taking orders and found out about the source of some of the problems they were encountering and why we were receiving complaints from customers.

"I then analyzed my findings and determined that the problem was a lack of sufficient coverage during peak hours and too much coverage during downtimes.

"I put together a small team to monitor and track calls and complaints.

"When I received the data from the team, I did some research on tracking systems. I talked to other customer service people in various companies and made some phone calls to get quotes.

"I wrote a proposal to my manager explaining the problem and made a recommendation to purchase a tracking system that would solve the problem.

"I met with my manager and laid out the problem with data, facts, and quotes. She was receptive to what I had found and the solution I had come up with.

"My manager and I then presented my report to upper management. I prepared a PowerPoint presentation that included a full report of the facts and figures and an estimate of the cost to improve the situation."

The interviewer has heard some key factors and skills that are needed for problem solving: analytical ability, research ability, the ability to make judgments and recommendations, and the ability to present and persuade, to name a few.

You've presented your story or example by walking through the specific steps you took to solve the problem. The interviewer is beginning to hear that you have the experience you claimed on your résumé. Remember, anyone can say that he or she is a good problem solver, but not everyone can give a specific example of a time when he or she solved a problem by providing specific details and facts as proof.

> **Rule 3.** Relate the results; in other words, tell how things turned out. Until you do this, the story is not finished. Ending the story is very important. If you leave out the results, the interviewer will be left wondering, "What happened? How did it turn out?" Your answer should include any results or feedback you received.

Answer's End

(Result)

"Upper management was very impressed with my presentation. There was some budget tweaking, but we got the green light to move forward. The new system is now in place, and orders have increased by 25 percent during peak hours. My boss was really delighted with me for finding the solution and putting together such a thorough package. I received the customer service award of a night on the town. I was really pleased."

This ending wraps up the example by indicating what improvements were made and how the company benefited as a result of your efforts. In this case, the company increased revenue through the use of a more efficient system. Note also that if you can quantify a result (a 25 percent increase in orders), it gives the interviewer the scope of your success. Another plus to this story is that it gave a quote or reaction from someone involved in the example: "My boss was really delighted." Any time you were rewarded, such as through a promotion, bonus, or award, that definitely should be included in your answer.

You can see from this example how much an interviewer can learn about the way you work from a single story. Because you structured the story chronologically, it's easier for the interviewer to understand the problem, your actions, and your results. Preparing your stories before the interview will allow you to put them in order and will make a tremendous difference in your ability to make an impact during the interview.

The Interviewer and Use of Behavioral Answers

When the interview is completed, the interviewer or interviewers will rate your answers and examples and evaluate you by using some sort of rating system. A sample evaluation might look like the one below, which uses a 5-point system in which each answer receives a specific point value. Each interviewer will rate your performance on the basis of the impression he or she acquired from your examples and stories.

Behavioral Interview Rating System

1. *Much more than acceptable (5 points).* Past experience is significantly above criteria required for successful performance.
2. *More than acceptable (3 points).* Past experience generally exceeds criteria relative to quality and quantity of behavior required.
3. *Acceptable (2 points).* Past experience meets criteria relative to quality and quantity of behavior required.
4. *Less than acceptable (1 point).* Past experience generally does not meet criteria relative to quality and quantity of behavior required.
5. *Much less than acceptable (no points).* Past experience is significantly below criteria required for successful job performance.

Each interviewer will add up the points awarded for each question, and a discussion will result (if the process has been done effectively). Your score is determined by what the interviewers hear in the answers you provide. If they are impressed by the stories you tell, they will rate you high: "much more than acceptable." If you have failed to give a specific example or back up your claims, they may rate you lower: "less than acceptable."

What you say during the interview is the only evidence the hiring manager can use to judge you at this point. Therefore, the more relevant and recent your stories are, the more of an impact they will have on the interviewer. When no experiences are related or if they happened more than 10 years ago, your score will be low. If you fail to tell your stories in an interesting and convincing manner, you may be rated low even though you may have the past experience necessary to perform well in the job.

Your stories and the way you relate them will be the key to convincing the interviewer that you are the right person for the job.

Other Interview Questions

Because not every interviewer is trained in behavioral interviewing techniques, you may be asked more general or traditional questions such as "What are your strengths and weaknesses?" If you develop your past success stories fully (see Step 3, "Writing Your Success Stories by Using Key Factors," you will feel better prepared and more confident about talking about yourself and will be able to answer almost any type of question.

What Is a Situational Question?

Situational Questions—Also Known as Traditional Questions: *"What Would You Do If . . . ?"*

Some interviews will focus more on situational questions such as "What would you do if you encountered a situation such as . . . ?" Here you essentially can make up an answer. Keep in mind, though, that even these answers will be stronger if you can give examples of times when you handled similar situations. The more information you can give the interviewer about yourself, the more accurate and reliable the picture of you that is being formed will be.

When you are asked a question such as "What would you do if . . . ?" you will know the interviewer is not looking for an example but wants to hear the way you think through a problem. In other words, the interviewer doesn't want to hear about past behavior and whether you have had the experience or not. Instead, he or she wants to know if you could handle a situation based on your thinking and judgment.

Although this type of questioning is not nearly as effective as using behavioral interview questions, some interviewers still use these questions. Understanding what the interviewer is looking for will help you be prepared to deal with this type of interview question. In these cases, you can spin a "tale" rather than tell a "story."

Situational questions would sound like the following:

Question. What would you do if you had a tight deadline with lots of priorities and deadlines?

Answer. I have a method of dealing with problems like this one.

By giving an example of how you think, you will intrigue the interviewer to want to hear more.

You can use the template below or make up your own way to remember, but it is a good idea to have a method to answer these "future behavior" questions. You could offer to give an example, but the interviewers may only want to see how you think through problems.

Using a template for situational questions will help you prepare to answer this type of question.

Template for Situational Questions

Situational questions are difficult to prepare for because they can be about any imaginable situation. When answering these questions, use your own natural way of solving problems. In fact, you can draw from a previous experience without telling a story or using a specific example. By using a template, you will be able to stay focused and succinct while describing your thinking process.

Here is an example of a template called *ERPIE*.

*E*valuate. Show how you seek information and details before you take action.

*R*esearch. Check for additional facts—what's been done in the past?

*P*lan. Develop the overall plan—action steps in detail.

*I*mplement. Put the plan in place, meeting any deadlines.

*E*valuate and Revaluate. Follow up on any promises and track outcomes.

Here are some examples of using the template.

Interviewer's Question

"What would you do if you were asked to coordinate a large event?"

Answer

"First I'd evaluate the purpose of the conference . . .

"Next I'd explore and research what has been done in the past—venue, type of things that worked, didn't work . . .

"I would also utilize any funds or people to use for a committee and then would delegate—food, entertainment, audiovisual, etc.

"I would put together a plan so that everyone knew what to do on the day of the conference.

"Because I am a detail person, I would make a checklist and go around the day of the conference.

"I'd have a list of everyone's contact info so that we could communicate the day of the event.

"I'd have several meetings, more as the event grew closer.

"I'd do a dry run to see if it went well.

"Last, I would evaluate and write recommendations for the next event of this type . . ."

The interviewer wants to know how you think through and deal with a problem, and so the more detail you give, the better.

Interviewer's Question

"What is the first thing you would do if you were given this position?" (*Hint:* You know that this specific job requires the use of communication skills, so why not start there?)

A Mediocre Answer

"First, I'd get to know the specific responsibilities of the other staff members. I'd talk with each of them and make sure that I learned what they did. Then I'd read as much as possible about the company and do research to learn what policies were implemented in the past. I'd also read the policy manual and find out the rules of the company. I'm sure that I would have a busy time just getting up to speed in the first 90 days or so."

There is really nothing wrong with this answer. It answers the question asked. The interviewer did not ask for a specific example or time. But note that the interviewer doesn't really get any concrete evidence of the way you work or the value of your skills at the conclusion of the answer. You gave a textbook answer, and that's all the interviewer has to go on when he or she judges whether you could do the job effectively and fit in at the company. At the same time—that's what was asked for.

Exercise: Putting Your Best Stories Forward

Think of a story you would like to tell an interviewer to let her or him know that you have had some past experiences. For this exercise, identify a specific time when you did something that you were especially pleased about or were commended or rewarded for doing. It doesn't have to be a big success, just something that you think would be of interest to the interviewer. Construct the story in its three parts:

1. *Beginning.* What the problem was. (Your examples must be specific, concise, and relevant to the question asked.)

2. *Middle.* What you did about the problem. (Your examples should include action, demonstrating your role. Don't just tell—show.)

3. *End (result).* How it turned out. (Your stories must have results or a conclusion.)

Eliminate the Negative

Go through your story and make sure it shows you in the best light by eliminating the following negative traits:

▶   Your examples should not be negative or whiny.

▶   Your examples should not bad-mouth anybody.

▶   Your examples should not be longer than three to four minutes.

▶   Your examples should not ramble about irrelevant details.

▶   Your examples should not include inappropriate language or slang.

▶   Your answers should not involve controversial subjects.

Step 2. Identifying the Key Factors of the Job

Every job has key factors or competencies that people at the company have identified as necessary or desirable in the person they hire to perform the duties of the job. Before you can write your success stories, you must determine what those key factors are so that you can tailor your résumé and the words you use to sell yourself to fit the requirements of the job. Reading through job postings and advertisements is one of the most effective ways to find out what employers are seeking in a candidate.

The Key Factors

One of the secrets of identifying these key factors is to begin to think like an interviewer. In the following sections, you will learn to identify these factors. Your task will be to identify the key skills necessary to do the job as if you were the person making the hiring decisions.

Thinking Like an Interviewer

Let's start by looking at a hypothetical job and deciding what key factors are desired for that job.

If a job description is well written, you can identify the skills required to do the job—beyond what is in the posting. Read through the job descriptions three times. The first time read for content and duties. The second time, read for words—vocabulary. (Note the language and words used to describe the job. It will be important in the interview to "talk the talk" of the industry, job, or company.) The third time you read through the description, think about what it would take to do the job—read between the lines.

In the example below, you'll find a description for a customer service representative. The specific requirements for the job are broken out one by one, followed by a number of skills or "key factors" needed for each requirement.

Example: Job Posting for a Customer Service Representative

When you are looking at a job posting, remember to look beyond what is written and consider the personal traits and transferable skills that will be needed to do this job.

General description. Customer service representatives are responsible for interaction with customers.

What will the job require you to do?

1. Provide information in response to inquiries about products and service and handle complaints through telephone interaction with customers.

    Skills and key factors for this requirement include:
    ▶ Communication skills
    ▶ Clear speaking style
    ▶ Listening skills
    ▶ Knowledge of products and services
    ▶ Knowledge of company policies and practices

2. Handle problems in a diplomatic manner and attempt to satisfy the customers' needs.

    Skills and key factors include:
    ▶ Interpersonal skills
    ▶ Ability to engage with the customer
    ▶ Ability to make the customer feel heard
    ▶ Patience and tact
    ▶ Follow-through
    ▶ Tolerance of people's behavior
    ▶ Ability to listen and identify the problem or error
    ▶ Ability to not take the complaints personally

3. Use good judgment before escalating the problem to the next level.

   Skills and key factors include:
   ▶ Common sense
   ▶ Judgment to recognize when to escalate
   ▶ Maturity to take responsibility

4. Keep records of customer interactions and transactions, recording details of inquiries, complaints, and comments, as well as actions taken.

   Skills and key factors include:
   ▶ Record-keeping skills
   ▶ Writing skills
   ▶ Attention to detail
   ▶ Organizational skills

Once you have identified the key factors, you will want to summarize those factors into five or more categories of skills. These categories will become the basis for deciding which stories to prepare for your interview.

Example of Identifying What Is Needed for This Position

Key factors needed for this job are:

Good communication skills—oral and written

Good interpersonal skills

Ability to deal with difficult people

Ability to not take complaints personally

Ability to deal with conflict

Ability to make judgments

Ability to take responsibility

Ability to write reports in a concise manner

We can summarize these into only a few main factors: the ability to communicate (written and orally), relate to others, evaluate and make judgments, take initiative, plan and organize, stay positive, and be self-motivating.

These are the factors to think about before the interview. Write stories of a time when you dealt with some or all of these factors. The more stories you write, the stronger your inventory will be to draw from during the interview. You may have to change the stories around according to the questions asked, but you will have your basic stories ready to go.

Exercise: Identifying Key Factors

It is now your turn to practice identifying key factors or competencies. Take a job description you have an interview for or go online and search to find jobs that would be of interest to you. Don't limit yourself geographically for this exercise—anything and everywhere goes. When you've selected a few jobs, print out the postings and practice identifying the key factors. The only qualifier in this exercise is that you would be interested in applying for the job.

What Are They Looking For?

What are the qualifications listed?

Break down each description line for line and identify the factors as in the example above.

▶ _____

▶ _____

▶ _____

▶ _____

▶ _____

What do you see that is needed? Remember to read between the lines. What would it take to succeed at this job?

▶ _____

▶ _____

▶ _____

▶ _____

▶ _____

Condense the factors you've identified into five or six words (e.g., *communication, adaptable, ability to influence, leadership*).

1. _____

2. _____

3. _____

4. _____

5. _____

6. _____

Note: These are the words and skills that should be emphasized on your résumé and in the interview to show that you are a perfect match for the position.

What Do You Have to Offer? Breaking Down Your Skills into Three Categories

Skills can be broken down into knowledge-based skills, transferable skills, and personal skills. Each category is discussed below.

KNOWLEDGE-BASED SKILLS

Some interviewers place the greatest emphasis on your knowledge and experience. Although this is not the best way to hire, it is a common practice. These skills usually are defined clearly in the job posting.

Take some time to identify your knowledge-based skills. Here are some examples:

Ability to analyze

Ability to estimate

Ability to coordinate

Negotiating skills

Organizational skills

Public speaking

Mechanical adeptness

Leadership skills

Counseling

Artistic skills

Computer skills

Entrepreneurial skills

Design skills

Budgeting skills

Training skills

Project management skills

TRANSFERABLE SKILLS

Transferable skills are skills that you can take to any job.

Identifying transferable skills is especially important for anyone who is changing careers or reentering the workforce after a time away. Think about what you have to offer in the way of transferable skills. Chances are that you are taking for granted some of the skills that make you unique.

Examples of transferable, or portable, skills include communication, planning, negotiating, organizational skills, time management, problem solving, customer service, teaching, coaching, follow-through, and resourcefulness.

Make your own list:

▶ _____

▶ _____

▶ _____

▶ _____

▶ _____

▶ _____

▶ _____

▶ _____

▶ _____

PERSONAL SKILLS

Personal skills are the qualities that make you unique—who you are.

These are skills that cannot be taught even though employers would like to do that. These skills are very important to outstanding job performance but sometimes are undervalued by both the candidate and the interviewer.

Think about your personal traits. Here are some examples: flexible, friendly, dependable, good attitude, reliable, calm, high energy, patient, self-starter, organized, quick learner, people oriented, goal directed, and good sense of humor.

Make your own list:

▶ _____

▶ _____

▶ _____

▶ _____

▶ _____

▶ _____

Exercise: Using the Three Ps

Divide a piece of paper into three columns and label the columns with the headings "Previous Experience and Education," "Portable Skills," and "Personality Traits," which stand for the three market Ps. This will be your marketing tool.

Previous Experience and Education

(*Examples:* vendor management, product development, computer expertise)

▶ _____

▶ _____

▶ _____

▶ _____

Portable (Transferable) Skills

(*Examples:* customer relations, communications, ability to coordinate, problem solving, time management)

▶ _____

▶ _____

▶ _____

▶ _____

▶ _____

▶ _____

▶ _____

Personality Traits

(*Examples:* self-starter, independent, friendly, organized, quick learner, good attitude)

▶ _____

▶ _____

▶ _____

▶ _____

▶ _____

▶ _____

When you finish, check the list to see a summary of what you have to offer. You may be surprised when you see how easily the list comes together. When you divide the skills, the task becomes manageable.

Take the key factors you identified from the job posting and compare them with what you have to offer. The next step is to plan a strategy to show off those traits in the stories and the answers you will prepare for the interview questions. It is now time to organize and prepare your stories involving past experiences so that when the time comes for the interview, you will convince the people making the hiring decisions that you are the best person for the job.

Step 3. Writing Your Success Stories by Using Key Factors

Storytelling consists of relating an incident or entertaining an audience with a tale. Some people consider storytelling an art form. In this section, we will expand on that idea. Using movie plots as an example of how a story unfolds to capture and hold the audience's attention, this section will show how the art of telling stories can be most effective.

Stories to Fit the Key Factors of the Job

By analyzing movie plots, you can see that almost all stories have a basic format that begins with a problem or obstacle, sometimes a formidable one. Then, at some point, usually in the first few minutes of the movie, the plot starts to thicken and the action begins. This is the part in which the characters attempt to deal with a situation or solve a problem, usually with some trials and tribulations and steps taken to move the plot forward while details are given to hold the viewers' attention. All good stories must have an ending: something that leaves the viewer with a feeling, positive or negative. The ending is always crucial to the story so that a solution can be seen—and in many cases a triumph over challenge can be achieved. You can use the same format to relate your professional success stories.

Using the plot of the classic movie *Indiana Jones and the Temple of Doom* as an example, let's examine how the storytelling process might work in your job search:

▶ *The beginning of the movie (the problem).* Indiana and his Chinese sidekick, an 11-year-old boy named Short Round, along with a gold-digging night club singer named Willie Scott, escape from a plane crash and sail down a river in an inflatable boat to a desolated village in India. The poor villagers believe the trio has been sent by a god to help them retrieve their kidnapped children and their stolen sacred stone from evil forces.

▶ *The plot or middle (the action).* Indiana and pals have quite an adventure encountering their enemies and outwitting them. There are several twists and turns, along with obstacles and challenges to overcome and survive. Indy is inspired by a sense of adventure and faces his own fears and is almost killed several times.

▶ *The ending (the result).* Indiana and his sidekicks survive and return the lost children and the stone to the natives.

You can see how this plot develops with a beginning, a middle, and an end. We are going to take this plot and write a story to show how your interview stories could evolve. Using Indiana as a job hunter, we'll show how his adventures prove that he is the right person for the job.

Posting on Craig's List

WANTED—Experienced adventurer extraordinaire. Seeking a fearless person to lead a diverse team on an unusual quest to achieve multiple goals. Must have an intense desire for adventure and have the ability be resourceful and determined. A knowledge of history and archaeology experience would be a plus.

Indiana knows this is the job for him and sends in his application. He is confident that he can handle anything thrown at him based on his past experience with the Temple of Doom.

He receives a call and is invited to come for an interview. Indiana is smart and does some preinterview preparation. The first thing he does is put together a list of key factors that he finds in the job posting. He carefully reads through the description and thinks about what it will take to do this job. As you did in Step 2, he reads between the lines and identifies six key factors:

▶ *Adaptability.* Experience in adapting to new situations and challenges

▶ *Team player.* The ability to work with diverse teams

▶ *Resourcefulness.* Good problem-solving skills—the ability to think outside the box

▶ *Leadership.* The ability to take the lead in overcoming and dealing with obstacles

▶ *Determination.* The will to persevere—does not give up in spite of the odds

▶ *Communication skills.* The ability to use and share past knowledge

Indy writes out his example stories using the formula of the beginning, the middle, and the end. By writing out the stories, he is making sure not to overdo the problem and to focus on the action. He now feels that he will be able to relate his stories to the interviewer as proof that he has what it takes to do the job. He feels prepared and confident as he enters the interviewer's office.

One of the first questions the interviewer asks is "Tell me about a time when you led an adventure with a team."

Indiana is ready with his answer:

▶ *Problem.* I recently had quite an adventure seeking the retrieval of kidnapped children and a precious stone that were stolen from poor villagers in India. There was an evil cult called the "Thuggees" whom my colleagues and I had to deal with to accomplish our goal to get back the children and the stone.

▶ *Action.* The first thing I did was to make a plan based on past knowledge as an archaeologist. I remained cool and calm in the face of some rather distressing situations. We entered the camp of the Thuggees, and at one point my colleagues and I were separated and I was drugged. But because of our strong teamwork, I was rescued by my sidekick Short Round, and we were able to rescue my other colleague from becoming a human sacrifice. I had to stay positive when we were trapped on a rope bridge over a gorge full of man-eating alligators. I made a calculated decision and took a risk when I cut the rope, leaving each of us clinging for our life to survive. I had to convince my colleagues that we were going to be OK and assure them that we could climb the rope—it took time and encouragement but we did it. When the leader of the Thuggees fell into the river, I was able to catch the sacred stone. We next set out to find the children, who were working in the mines.

▶ *Result.* My colleagues and I were able to free the imprisoned children and take them and the stone back to the villagers. Needless to say, we were instant heroes.

The interviewer is impressed with Indiana's story and the skills he describes.

▶ *Adaptability.* Having been saved, he was immediately ready to take on a new task: to find the children and the sacred stone.

▶ *Team player.* He worked with and supported other team members, staying positive and motivating them in the face of death.

▶ *Resourcefulness.* He found several means to survive and to retrieve the stone and the children.

- *Leadership.* He assumed the role of leader from the beginning and was steadfast.
- *Determination.* He was a survivor in spite of overwhelming odds—being drugged, trapped on a rope bridge with alligators waiting to eat him.
- *Communication skills.* He worked together with his colleagues, encouraging them when needed for survival.

By relating his earlier success stories, Indiana has let the interviewer know about the skills he can bring to the job. Using additional prepared stories, Indiana is able to prove to the interviewer that he is the best person for the job. His past behavior is an indicator of his future success, and he is hired!

From Indiana's experience, you can see that preparation does pay off. A well-told example helps the interviewer match your qualifications to the employer's needs. The interviewing process gives you an opportunity to tell your stories and your triumphs over challenges so that the interviewer can use patterns of behavior to determine whether you have what it takes to get the job done. The main objective of the story is to relate your strengths and skills through past experiences and behaviors. The more interesting and relevant your stories are to the job, the more impressive they will be at demonstrating that you have been there and done that—and can do it again.

Begin to think of your stories as "tales" of past experiences. As you already know, all good tales have a beginning, a middle, and an ending.

The beginning. There was a time . . . (the situation)

The middle. The plot and steps taken, the challenges and obstacles . . . (the action)

The ending. The outcome (how it turned out)

Using Acronyms as a Guide

One of the challenges of writing and telling success stories is to tell them in a succinct and organized manner. Your story should unfold in a chronological sequence, making it easy for the listener to follow it and learn additional information about you and the way you work.

You may be familiar with the concept of using an acronym—a term formed from the first letter of each word in a series of words—to remember items in a sequential manner. In fact, we already used one previously when we talked about ERPIE—which, if you recall, stands for *evaluate, research, plan, implement,* and *evaluate* and re-evaluate. An acronym not only gives your memory a jog but also provides a format and structure for you to follow. When it comes to interviewing, several acronyms are used to tell stories, some of which you may have encountered in other books you have read or courses you have attended. Some of the more commonly used acronyms in storytelling are the following:

CAB

Challenge. The problem you had to overcome

Action. The techniques and skills you used to accomplish your goal

Behavior. Your behavior relative to this situation

PAR

Problem. The reason you did it

Action. Your response—what you did

Result. The outcome—what happened

SAR

Situation. The problem

Action. The steps you took

Result. The outcome

STAR

Situation or task. The background of the action

Action. The response—what was done

Result. The effects of the action

SBO

Situation. The situation you encountered

Behavior. The behavior used

Outcome. The way it turned out—successes or failures

SAO

Situation. A description of the situation

Action. The actions you took

Outcome. The results

SPARE

Situation or problem. A succinct description of the challenge

Action. The detailed role you took

Result. The results, rewards, and comments received

Enthusiasm. Your reaction to or feeling about the situation

The common pattern in these acronyms is the chronological order they use to relate the events: a beginning, a middle, and an ending.

You can use these acronyms as a template when you are writing or telling your stories to make them clearer, more focused, and more sequential, but it is also important to understand that you should use certain proportions to get the impact you want.

The Proportions of a Story

You may have noticed when you were answering the questions in the Interview IQ Test that some of the answers were not as strong as others because the emphasis was in the wrong place. In other words, the stories were out of proportion. Some of the stories placed too much emphasis on the problem and not enough on the action. Some had a good beginning and middle but lacked a conclusion or outcome. By breaking down the story into specific proportions, you will keep the focus on your skills and experiences, not on the company or the problem.

Mistakes of Proportion

A common mistake candidates make is not giving enough detail in the action of the story. If you do not include the action steps or the details of what you did, the listener cannot get a clear picture of the skill sets you used to achieve the result. By spending too much time on the beginning or the ending, you are missing an opportunity to let interviewers know that you have done what they are looking for in similar situations in your earlier jobs.

What are some other mistakes candidates make? Here are three common ones:

▶ Too much time is given to setting up the story.
▶ Not enough information is provided in the middle of the story. The action is simplified, making it sound like it was an easy task or problem when in fact it was very difficult and it involved a great deal of effort above and beyond the norm.

▶ The story does not have an ending. What was the outcome? The interviewer is left wondering, "What happened next?"

Your Story

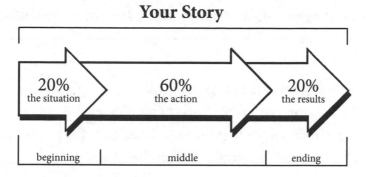

20%	60%	20%
the situation	the action	the results
beginning	middle	ending

The Right Proportions

The proportions you want to follow to create the most effective story are these:

The beginning—20 percent or less. The situation, task, or problem. (Five to seven sentences)

The middle—60 percent or more. The action, the steps taken to solve the problem: ideas generated, tasks performed, challenges overcome—your role in the process. (Seven to nine steps taken)

The ending—20 percent or less. The results: cost savings, bonuses, awards, promotions—the outcome. (Three to five sentences)

Examples of Story Proportions

Using the correct proportions for a story is essential in getting your points across in a succinct manner. When you spend too much or too little time on one part, the story does not have the power it could have. Below are two examples of behavioral questions and answers. One is a poor example, and the other is a good example.

A Poorly Told Story

Interviewer's Question

"Tell me about a time when you dealt with a dissatisfied customer."

Answer

Beginning. "That is the nature of my job: dealing with dissatisfied customers. I probably get an average of 25 calls each day from people who aren't satisfied with the products, have a broken product, want information on how to return the product, or need information about how to operate the product. They call and yell at us, thinking it is our responsibility. It's like they think we are empowered to do something about the problem. We have a policy at ABC to always try to satisfy the customer."

Middle. No action.

Ending. "We even go so far as to refund money in some cases. Other companies would not be so generous, but our company really cares about its reputation."

This story has problems with the proportions and as a result lacks order and effectiveness:

▶ Too much emphasis is on the problem (more than 20 percent of the story).
▶ No identifiable skills are given (no action).
▶ The end is focused on what the company does, not on the skills and knowledge you possess. A good way to end a story is with a kudo or comment from another person.

A Well-Told Story

Interviewer's Question

"Tell me about a time when you dealt with a dissatisfied customer."

Answer

Beginning. "In my last job, a female customer called with a complaint about an order we had shipped incorrectly. She was very upset and started yelling at me."

Middle. "The first thing I did was listen very carefully and let her vent. I talked to her in a quiet tone, making sure I was polite but not condescending. When she had calmed down, I asked her to explain the details of the situation. I then repeated the problem back to her and confirmed that I understood all the details. I assured her that I would call her back that day. I did some research on the problem and the circumstances. After I had the facts, I discussed the situation with my supervisor. I made a recommendation that we adjust the customer's bill on the basis of my findings, and my supervisor agreed."

Ending. "I called the woman back that day, as promised, and told her what we could do to make it up to her. She was very receptive to our offer and felt satisfied with the adjustment. She asked to speak to my supervisor and told her about my excellent and professional customer service."

You don't have to be a trained interviewer to see the difference between these two stories. The first story is very vague and incomplete, with too little emphasis on the action and too much emphasis on the beginning (the problem). The interviewer will have a difficult time judging what the candidate has to offer at the conclusion of this story. What skills could you pick out? Not many.

The second story is very specific and points out several qualities an interviewer is looking for in an employee who will be dealing with customers. The story is easy to follow and has appropriate proportions: 20 percent for the beginning, 60 percent for the middle, and 20 percent for the ending.

Exercise: Identifying Skills

Reread the second story and identify the skills you can draw from it. List them below:

_____

_____

_____

_____

Here are some of the skills you might have identified in the well-told story:

Good listening skills

Communication skills

Follow-through

Research

Fact-finding skills

Initiative

Problem-solving skills

If you were the interviewer and picked out even some of these skills, would you want to hear more from this candidate? Probably you would, especially if these are the skills you identified as important to the position.

Once you feel comfortable with the concept and proportions of storytelling, try retaking the Interview IQ Test to improve your score.

Your Success Stories

Writing success stories is one of the most important steps in preparing for an interview. The first step in the process is to determine which factors are crucial to the position for which you are applying (you learned how to do this in Step 2). Once you have determined the skills and competencies that are required, the next step is to write your own experience stories that emphasize those factors.

A common problem in writing stories involves the use of pronouns. You easily can get tangled in pronouns and miss out on the opportunity to explain your role in the story. When you use too many *we*s, it is difficult, if not impossible, for the interviewer to know your role in the situation.

Here is an example:

> "We had a problem with the database we were working on, and we had to do a quick analysis to determine the cause. The first thing we did was analyze the previous data. We found the flaw within a few minutes, and we were able to solve the problem in record time."

This example has six *we*s and no *I*s. What was your role? You got lost in the example somewhere. There is no proof of your performance in the story; this means that you have missed an opportunity to show the interviewer your skill sets.

If you are worried about using the pronoun *I* too many times, talk about the team you worked with, but at the same time include your role and what you did. Here is an example:

> "I worked with a team, and my role was to do the analysis on the product. We got together, and each person presented his or her findings. I found that there was a basic error in the system and was able to work with the engineer to reconfigure the problem."

The strong point in this story is that there is a sense of what your role was on the team. You didn't take the credit for the solution but showed that you played a role in the solution.

Exercise: Creating the Story Line

It is now time for you to write your own success stories so that you can let the interviewer know you are the best person for the job. You can do this by following four logical steps.

The first step is to determine which factors are crucial to the position. Once you have determined what skills and competencies are required, you can begin to write experience stories that address your experience in the identified areas.

Here is an example:

- ▶ Communication
- ▶ Decision making
- ▶ Initiative
- ▶ Planning and organizing
- ▶ Flexibility
- ▶ Leadership

Second, on the basis of these requirements, formulate at least two possible questions for each of the six factors. (Refer to the Interview IQ Test in Part 1 for examples of questions.) Some sample questions include the following:

"Tell me about a time when your communication skills made a difference in the outcome of a project."

"Can you give me an example of a time when you had to break down complex terms into simple language to communicate to a group?"

Third, for each key factor or job requirement, prepare at least two stories that illustrate your successes and answer the questions you have formulated.

The fourth and final step is to review your stories to see which examples are interchangeable and can be used to answer more than one direct question.

Exercise: Writing Your Own Stories

In this exercise, you'll be writing out your own stories, making sure the story proportions are right. You may find it easier to do this exercise if you use the acronym SPARE.

Situation or Problem: The Beginning (20 Percent or Less)

What is the basis of the story? State the situation or problem at the beginning of the story. The beginning should be brief and concise.

There was a time when I encountered a problem with . . .

_____

_____

Action (or Behavior): The Middle (60 Percent or More)

Describe what you did to address the problem. List your actions. (Beware of the pronoun *we*, which can take attention away from your part in the action). This part of the story should include movement and details.

I worked with a team, and my role was . . .

_____

_____

Some of the steps I took were . . .

_____

_____

The biggest challenge on this project was . . .

_____

_____

And then what I did was . . .

_____

_____

Result: The End or Outcome (20 Percent or Less)

What was the outcome or ending to the story? Focus on your role in the project and any feedback you received.

The result was . . .

_____

_____

The feedback I received was . . .

_____

_____

_____

Enthusiasm

End with some comments about your reaction to or feelings regarding the success of the situation or task.

The most rewarding part of this situation was . . .

_____

_____

_____

The biggest challenge for me was . . .

_____

_____

_____

What Not to Say

Ideally, your stories will demonstrate your abilities and successes. When you have been involved in a project that did not turn out the way it was planned but the end results had nothing to do with your performance (e.g., money ran out, customer canceled the order), you should focus on what your role was and how you fulfilled your task in the project. In other words, focus on what you were responsible for and how that part turned out.

Important Details to Include and Unimportant Details to Exclude

Some of the ugly details of a story can be skipped over without taking attention away from your role in the situation. It is important to focus on the positive as much as possible during an interview.

It is in your best interest not to say anything negative about a company or boss in your stories. Remember, these are professional stories and you are demonstrating that you are a professional and the best person for the job.

Your stories should be as upbeat and interesting as possible. From the interviewer's perspective, hiring a new employee can be a very intense and somewhat tedious task. It is a task that a lot of managers would rather not have to perform because it involves talking to a great many people and listening to their experiences and the details of those experiences. However, when someone comes into the interview and begins to tell interesting stories, the interview becomes enjoyable and sometimes even fun. By engaging the interviewer with your stories, you will have a better chance of being remembered and thought of as a serious candidate for the job.

Your vocabulary and the words you use will tell the interviewer a lot about you. Be sure to familiarize yourself with the jargon of the industry. This will allow you to discuss problems and issues in a more intelligent manner.

The more at ease you are with what the interviewer is seeking and the closer a match you are to what the employer is looking for, the better chance you have of being selected and receiving a job offer.

Step 4. Understanding the Keys to Success

Preparation

As has been stressed throughout Part 2, preparation will make a definite difference in your presentation and confidence during the interview. One of the biggest mistakes job seekers make is not preparing well enough for a job interview. You must convey confidence about your skills and ability to do the job to let the interviewer know that you are the best person for the job—the solution to the problem.

The most successful interviews are ones that are conversational, involving an exchange between two professionals. For some people, this may entail a paradigm shift in the way they think about an interview. However, if you do think in this new way, you will see greater results, experience a significant gain in confidence, have less fear, and get over some of your nervousness about the process. In an interview, the worst possible position for a candidate to take is "Please, please, hire me." This not only is a weak and passive position but also renders you powerless, and it is boring for the interviewer. Taking the following steps will help you gain greater confidence and give stronger answers.

1. Stop thinking of the interview process as a hockey game and begin thinking of it as a two-way conversation between two professionals.
2. Start thinking of the process as a business solution process in which the employer has a problem and you, the candidate, are the solution to that problem.

The necessary shift in the interview process entails changing from the defensive position of responding to questions with the answers you think the interviewer wants to hear to thinking of the process as two or more people getting together to check each other out.

Centering your preparation on who you are as a product and what that product has to offer will change the focus of your preparation and presentation. To prepare for interviews, use the Interview IQ Test as a guide and complete all the exercises in this book. Doing that will give you a much stronger sense of what you have to offer and what makes you unique so that you can sell yourself on the basis of what you can offer the employer.

A self-assessment of your skills and traits is essential before you can think about yourself as a product. The more details you have about your skill sets, the more effectively you will be able to present yourself as the solution to the employer's problem (i.e., the best person for the job).

List not only your knowledge and experience from former positions but also some of your transferable skills as well as your personal traits, which are important factors for success in any job. By identifying the key factors of the position and then basing your stories on the competencies identified, you will be taking the most essential step in your preparation.

Focusing your preparation on what the employer is seeking will make a big difference in the way you communicate, especially when it comes to asking questions. By printing out several postings (the only criterion being that you would be interested in applying, not that you necessarily will apply), you will begin to be familiar with the requirements of the jobs in your field as well as the vocabulary used.

Take the words and use them to enhance your credibility. The words you use to express yourself send a strong message about who you are and what you know. What words you use and how well you use them say more about you than does the message you're trying to communicate.

Practice, Practice, Practice

Interviewing is a learned skill. As with any other skill or learned technique, the more you practice, the more you will improve. You will find that receiving objective feedback on how you are coming across will help you be more effective. When you can listen objectively to any advice or critique you receive, you will learn a lot about the impression you are making. No one likes being criticized, but this is a time when you need to know whether you are sending the right message and making the impression you intend to make.

Here are some methods to use for getting feedback. Keep in mind that some may be more effective for you than others are.

Actual Interviews

Using interviews to get feedback is a method that can be very costly. You can use job interviews that are not of great importance as practice if you have the opportunity, but that can backfire if you discover that this would be a better opportunity for your career than you originally thought. You may discover that when you are not concerned about whether you get the job, you may interview at your best because you don't have anything to lose. Take that attitude toward interviews into the interviews for jobs that you really want and you will have greater success.

Feedback is important, but getting the interviewer to give you feedback after you have been turned down is not easy. Most interviewers are concerned about saying the wrong thing and ending up being subject to some kind of a discrimination claim. Every once in a while someone will take the time to tell you where you could have been more effective and convincing. If you are fortunate enough to receive this type of feedback, keep an open mind and listen as objectively as possible. Learn from the experience.

Self-Coaching

Record and listen to yourself. Although this technique may be challenging, try to be as objective as possible about what you hear. Try putting the recording away for a day or so before you play it back; this will help you be more objective. When you are ready, listen to the recording with an open mind. While you listen, ask yourself, "If I were the interviewer, would I hire me?"

Career Centers

If you have access to a career center through a school, government-sponsored organization, or private organization, take the opportunity to work with trained professionals who will give you feedback about the impression you are making.

Practice with a Friend or Family Member

This is a good way to practice as long as some ground rules have been established. However, it can be a disaster if it is not handled correctly. People who are close to you are often not in a good position to critique your performance as objectively as would someone who doesn't know you. Your friends and family members are emotionally involved and on your side. They may not want to say anything negative about your interviewing skills. Make sure to agree beforehand that the session will be limited to objective advice and then try to listen without taking it personally and getting your feelings hurt.

Professional Coaching

Use a coach, but not just any coach. Make sure she or he has had interview training, particularly in behavioral interviewing techniques. Qualify the coach by asking about the last time he or she was on an interview and about his or her experiences as an interviewer. Make sure the coach has sat on both sides of the desk and ask for references from past clients.

Whatever method you choose, it is essential to practice, practice, and practice some more. Any feedback you receive should be listened to in as objective a mindset as possible. This is not a time to be aggressive and argumentative. Don't take it personally but instead learn from the experience. Your goal should be to sound not rehearsed but prepared and natural.

There are so many factors behind the scenes of the hiring process, it is impossible to judge why one interview ends in a job offer and one does not. What is possible to predict is that if you go to an interview and try to wing your answers, you will be less focused and feel less confident and will give the interviewer a weak picture of you.

Feeling confident is the most important trait you can show at an interview. If you believe in yourself and know you can do the job, you will be able to project that confidence. If you use phrases such as "pretty good," "think I can," and "probably could," you will not convince the interviewer that you are the "best person for the job." This is not a time to be modest; it is a time to sell yourself as the solution to the problem. Any statement you make should be made with conviction.

TIP Leave your modesty at the door—and bring your heart into the interview—be yourself.

Interviewer's Question

"What makes you think you can do this job?

Answer

"I am a very good match for this position and have the traits you are looking for. Through my past experiences, I have encountered the challenges necessary to do this job. I am known for my ability to learn quickly and come up to speed in record time. I know I can make a difference in this department. I haven't ever set a goal yet that I didn't achieve. I've been there and done that—and can do it again for you!"

The Interview IQ Test gives you a look at the interviewing process from the other side of the desk. It is your entry into the world of the interviewer. The strength of the answers given there will help you gauge the effectiveness of your answers. Use the test as a learning tool and guide, and use it over and over. Learn from the mistakes of the weaker answers as well as from the strengths of the stronger answers.

By taking the Interview IQ Test several times and perhaps reviewing it before every interview, you will have a stronger sense of what an interviewer is seeking when he or she says, "Give me an example of a time when . . ." By familiarizing yourself with behavioral interviewing techniques, you will be prepared to back your claims even when you are not asked for an example.

Once you have done the exercises and prepared your own stories, you will have a passport to successful interviewing. It will be up to you to prepare and practice until you have the skill perfected and are ready to go out to the next interview with cool, calm, and confidence.

Rules of Behavioral Interviewing

▶ Your examples must be specific.
▶ Your examples should be concise.
▶ Your examples of action should be the focus of the story—what you did.
▶ Your examples must demonstrate your role.
▶ Your examples should be relevant to the questions asked.
▶ Your stories must have results.

Boost your Interview IQ and show the interviewer that you are the best person for the job!

PART III

Management and Executives

As a manager or an executive, you may have had a great deal of experience with interviewing—at least as the interviewer. It may have been some time since you sat on the other side of the desk as the candidate. Even the most savvy professionals have been known to get nervous about the interview, especially if they have not interviewed in a long time.

Taking the Interview IQ Test may serve as a brush-up or possibly provide you with a new perspective on how to answer some questions in the strongest manner possible. Interviewing for a job can be a humbling experience for the most confident of managers. Even the most confident candidates have been known to get dry mouth and that fluttery feeling in the stomach—so it's normal to get those feelings. In fact, those feelings are the same feelings that many famous people experience when they are about to perform. This is all the more reason to do some preparation and to practice your answers and not wing the interview cold.

Taking the interview quiz may act as a reminder of the basics and may bring back memories of some experiences you may not have thought about in a long time. It will also give you an up-to-date look at interviewing techniques such as behavioral interviewing or performance-based interviewing. The interviewer wants to hear what you've done in the past in order to judge your pattern of operation or behavior in the future. If you've done it before, you can do it again.

The Interview IQ Test:
Management and Executives Questions

INTERVIEWER'S QUESTION

[1] "Let's begin by your telling me about yourself."

Select the strongest answer.

[A] I have been in the sales business for over 20 years now and have worked in a variety of companies and held a number of positions. My success has happened primarily because I know how to build relationships. I show a genuine interest in my customers and in turn built trust. In fact, I have customers that I have known for as long as 9 or 10 years.

I take my job very seriously and do whatever it takes to drive revenue. I know what it takes to build profit margins, and as you may have seen on my résumé, I have some great results in my jobs. I believe in service not only to acquire new customers but to keep the customers that have been loyal and have come to depend on me as their contact.

[B] I have 10 years of experience working in the HR Management. I started in this business when things were basically very different with regard to technology, and I have continued my education to continue to stay on top of the latest trends and programs used to track various aspects of employee policies and benefit changes. As you can see from my résumé, I have a broad knowledge in several areas in HR, ranging from Performance Management to Recruiting.

[C] I have 20 years of experience working in the HR field. I have held a variety of roles with increased responsibility in each job. As you may have noticed from my résumé, I have a broad knowledge of several areas in HR, ranging from Talent Management and Culture Change to Change Management and Recruiting.

For the past 9 years I have been responsible for succession planning for top executives to ensure continuity of leadership. My strength is my analytical problem-solving ability. I am able to break down problems, define the key issues, and implement plans. I have a very high work ethic and am known for remaining calm under pressure. I am strategic in my team approach, asking a group to step back and see beyond the horizon while showing them how to connect the dots. My approach is "high involvement" of all players. I don't believe in making decisions in a vacuum.

ANSWERS

The Strongest Answer

[**C**] This is the strongest answer because it answers the question "Tell me about yourself." There is a combination of experiences and facts: information about you and how you have succeeded at your job. By combining your experience and successes with your personal traits and skills, the interviewer will grasp a better picture of who you are and how your various experiences have prepared you to take on this responsibility. This is especially true if you are lacking in some area of expertise.

The Mediocre Answer

[**A**] This answer is OK but would be stronger if it were more specific. For instance "my success" would be a stronger statement if it said what your success was. Example: "In every job I have ever held I have doubled the sales within one year's time." Another example is saying "I have had some great results in my jobs." This would be a stronger statement if it were specific about the "great results": "I increased sales and/or profits and customer retention." More specific information is needed. The more specific the description of your success, the more impressed the interviewer will be with your past experience. The interviewer may want to hear more examples to see if there is a pattern of behavior.

The Weakest Answer

[**B**] The reason this answer is the weakest is because it reveals very little about you as a person. It is unfeeling and somewhat cold. Remember, the question was "Tell me about yourself," not "Walk me through your résumé." Several qualities are talked about, but the interviewer doesn't get any specifics without digging deeper. Interviewers will give up if the information given is not relevant to answering the question.

RATE YOURSELF

If you chose answer [**C**], give yourself 5 points.

If you chose answer [**A**], give yourself 3 points.

If you chose answer [**B**], give yourself 0 points.

INTERVIEWER'S QUESTION

[2] "Give me a specific example of a time when you took the initiative."

Select the strongest answer.

[A] When I took over the department in my last job, there were turnover problems. I sat down with the staff members and asked them why so many people were leaving. I learned that when they were hired, they were told that there would be cross-functional training, but it never happened. I consider my team to be my main customer, and I immediately set a plan in motion. It involved presenting my plan to top management and requesting extra time and money. I put my job on the line, but I got what we needed. I turned the department around and bought some strong loyalty from my staff.

[B] I attempted to initiate things in my last company, but nobody was really interested in what I had to say. I always volunteer and am glad to help in any way that I can, but I don't want to take the responsibility for initiating projects. The last time I initiated something for a company, I got stuck with all the responsibility and work. I gave up trying to do something other than my job. Don't get me wrong. I am a hard worker and am more than willing to pull my weight, but I let other people lead.

[C] This is an example from my life outside of my job, but it is a project that I am very proud of. I was responsible for initiating a clothing drive for the homeless in our city. It came about when we were talking at lunch one day. There is a woman who hangs out near our building, and we all felt sorry for her because it was getting cold. Some of us had clothes and blankets that we were glad to donate, but we didn't know exactly how to approach the situation. I volunteered to research the situation and set up a drive. Some of my coworkers volunteered to help. By the end of the month, we had collected so many coats and blankets that we presented them to the city for the shelters. We got a commendation from the mayor, and we all felt really good about what we did.

ANSWERS

The Strongest Answer

[**A**] This is the strongest answer because it is a specific example and does a good job of showing how you stepped up to the plate and initiated action—how you got things done. This is an effective example of being a good leader who takes the time to listen and respond. It is also an answer that shows strong qualities for motivating others and handling groups.

The Mediocre Answer

[**C**] This answer has all the right proportions of a good story. It is a good example of what you can do if you don't have a work-related experience to talk about. It is a great example of a volunteer or personal situation. Any story is better than no story to demonstrate the quality or skill you are trying to show. In this case, you took the initiative to set up and research a program to help others, which is an admirable thing to do.

The Weakest Answer

[**B**] This is the weakest answer because it is not specific. It's the tone, though, that is really the weakest part of this response. It sounds negative and angry. It's not so much what is said but the impression it gives. If you don't want to lead, that is acceptable, but try to focus on the positive side of what you've done in the interview. Negative attitudes are a real turnoff for interviewers.

RATE YOURSELF

If you chose answer [**A**], give yourself 5 points.

If you chose answer [**C**], give yourself 3 points.

If you chose answer [**B**], give yourself 0 points.

INTERVIEWER'S QUESTION

[3] "Describe your leadership or management style."

Select the strongest answer.

[A] My style is "bottom-line driven." The customer is the most important product and the one who makes it possible to pay the bills. It's a numbers game. The more customers you have, the more revenue is generated. I believe in customer service. I believe in empowering my team to do whatever it takes to satisfy the customer. I believe that if you have a solid customer base, you will have a profitable business.

[B] I lead by example. I work hard and meet deadlines, and I expect my subordinates to do the same thing. I don't mind assisting when there are problems, but I don't believe in holding anyone's hand through projects. I assign the work and expect that the work will get done. If I have to look over shoulders to keep people on schedule, I am not a good manager. My preferred style in a boss is the "hands-off" approach. Just give me an assignment and let me go to work.

[C] If you asked my team members, they would tell you that I am a fair and open manager. I make myself available every day. My objective is to recognize people for their strengths. I recently promoted a team member who had begun as a problem employee but through some one-on-one coaching from me, along with his willingness to put in some extra time, he was able to become a star.

ANSWERS

The Strongest Answer

[**C**] This is strongest answer because it gives a specific example and an indirect endorsement from your team. These are good techniques to use when you are answering a subjective question like this one. This answer demonstrates a genuine commitment to supporting the team members and to letting them know that their work counts in the bigger picture—and it provides a specific example of how you do that.

The Mediocre Answer

[**A**] This answer would work at a company that is about the bottom line and only that. Although many companies are bottom-line driven, they are usually known as sweat shops, where they use and abuse their employees. There is no doubt that money and profit are important to keep a business afloat, but this answer does not show a basic understanding of leadership. It certainly addresses where the management focus is: making money through customers. However, it does not address the internal customer: the worker or the team.

The Weakest Answer

[**B**] This answer shows a very hands-off approach to management, which might be OK depending on what the position requires and what the company is looking for. "Give them the work and let them struggle" is the message here. The job description will be key to deciding which factor should be emphasized—independence or collaboration. The most important point is that the management style preferred by the company is the same as your preferred style. You will perform best if there is a good fit here.

RATE YOURSELF

If you chose answer [**C**], give yourself 5 points.

If you chose answer [**A**], give yourself 3 points.

If you chose answer [**B**], give yourself 0 points.

INTERVIEWER'S QUESTION

[4] "Describe a time when you had to make an unpopular decision."

Select the strongest answer.

[A] In my job as a project manager, I worked with a team of technicians, and it was my task to find cost-cutting measures. This included laying off personnel. I labored over my decision to make sure that I was being objective. I analyzed each person and his or her role in the project. In the end, I was asked to cut head count by 20 percent. I prepared my list based on my careful planning. I was the one who had to tell people that their jobs were being cut. I felt I had treated the situation as fairly as I could, but I must admit it was a very tough task to announce the layoffs to my staff.

[B] There was a time when I decided to hire an external candidate for a job that several internal candidates had applied for. Many people were upset with my decision and let me know about it. In fact, one person actually was upset enough to go to human resources and claim that she was discriminated against. I defended my decision to people who complained and tried to justify my decision. I had to do what I felt was in the best interest of the department. I felt like I had picked an excellent candidate and stood by my decision.

[C] Sometimes a manager has to make unpopular decisions. That's what we get paid to do—to think outside the box and make decisions. I've made some difficult decisions over my career, and some were the right decisions and some the wrong decisions. If I think something is wrong, I will let you know about it. I'm not a person who lets things pile up. I try to act on the problem as soon after it happens as possible.

ANSWERS

The Strongest Answer

[**A**] This is a great example of a time when a tough decision had to be made. You can hear that although telling people that their jobs were over was not pleasant, you handled it through an objective process. The tone of the answer indicates that this was done in a very careful and caring manner. It also shows proactive preparation with the planning of the task. In addition, this answer demonstrates strength in your ability to do whatever it takes to get the job done.

The Mediocre Answer

[**B**] This answer does not give any specifics. You made the decision but left some facts unknown: Why did you made the decision or what criteria did you use to justify not hiring the internal candidates? What made you hire the external candidate? The story would be stronger if you told how you justified your decision and what criteria you used to rule out the internal candidates. Also, the answer doesn't include an outcome. Did your decision make things better for the department, the company, or your overall standing with the team?

The Weakest Answer

[**C**] This is the weakest answer because it does not address the question. It starts out with a statement and then carries that statement throughout the answer. The interviewer might become concerned by "some were the wrong decisions." You want to stay upbeat and positive, or it will leave the wrong impression.

RATE YOURSELF

If you chose answer [**A**], give yourself 5 points.

If you chose answer [**B**], give yourself 3 points.

If you chose answer [**C**], give yourself 0 points.

INTERVIEWER'S QUESTION

[5] "Tell me about a time when you had to link long-range visions and strategies to day-to-day work."

Select the strongest answer.

[A] That would be my experience with branding. We hired some star athletes to "brand" our product. We sold the brand name, and everything we did pushed the name. We bought focused lists and sent out thousands of ads through e-mail. We spent a fair share of our budget pushing the brand. Every activity revolved around this brand we were trying to establish. Everyone in the company bought into the concept. The result was overwhelmingly successful, and the team received many kudos.

[B] A challenge that I faced when I started at my last company was a lack of customer retention. I worked closely with my staff and members of other relevant departments to strategize ways to retain first, build second. Teams were sent out to conduct focus groups and interview current customers. I worked closely with the marketing department to analyze the data. As a result, the way we did business with customers was to use "permission marketing," asking first, sending only upon request for information. The key to the success of this program was getting buy-in from the members of my team and then giving them all my support from the very beginning.

[C] I usually keep up with what's going on in the general market and sometimes have to act fast to get market share. One time in particular, we were trying to get attention in a fast-paced environment. I usually spend a great deal of work around budget, attempting to maximize leverage. I've been known to buy some premium advertising to get the word out. I've led some successful campaigns, even when market conditions have not been in our favor. I really know what I'm doing out there, and the results are the proof.

ANSWERS

The Strongest Answer

[**B**] This is the strongest answer. The answer is specific to a particular project. It tells the story from the beginning, allowing it to unfold in a "storytelling" style. This is a behavioral question that is looking for an example of how you have worked in the past, since past behavior is an indicator of future success. The example indicates your ability to see details and work with individuals across functions while maintaining the big-picture perspective.

The Mediocre Answer

[**C**] This answer does not cite a specific project, and so it does not address the question. It mentions "One time in particular" but then goes off on a tangent about past behavior in a broad sense. It then sounds like bragging rather than telling about accomplishments. One of the keys to good interviewing is to listen to what is asked for by the interviewer. Only then can you answer the question correctly.

The Weakest Answer

[**A**] This is the weakest answer because it does not talk about your role. If you look back at the answer, you can count six *we*s and no *I*s. Although it is important to show a strong team function, there should also be some sign of *you* and your part in the planning and implementation. What was your role, and how did you implement and lead the team?

RATE YOURSELF

If you chose answer [**B**], give yourself 5 points.

If you chose answer [**C**], give yourself 3 points.

If you chose answer [**A**], give yourself 0 points.

INTERVIEWER'S QUESTION

[6] "In what ways has your current or last job prepared you to take on more responsibility?"

Select the strongest answer.

[A] I have had extensive experience working with customers in my last job. In the beginning, I had to learn to deal with people who were very frustrated and wanted to take their feelings out on me. I have to admit that in the beginning it really would get to me when someone was being nasty and rude. Since that time, I've taken some training courses on selling and human behavior that have helped immensely. I needed that experience to be able to move forward to a job like this one.

[B] My current job is really not a good fit for me. I am overqualified and somewhat bored. I took the job knowing that I could do it without much of a stretch. The job before this one was a real burnout type of environment, and I needed a job that was kind of low key. I am now ready to move forward and give my all to this job. I know I could do this job and bring added value to the department.

[C] My last job was a great stepping-stone for me to take on the new challenges this job will provide. I had to deal with all kinds of situations and people in my last job. After five years in that job, I am ready for some new challenges in a new industry. I know I am ready to move up and would be good at this job because I have the patience needed to deal with difficult people.

ANSWERS

The Strongest Answer

[**A**] This is the strongest answer because it clearly gives an example of growth and experience. It also talks about training and development to get an understanding beyond the job itself. This is a good example of showing how your past experience is an indicator of your future success.

The Mediocre Answer

[**C**] This is not a bad answer, but it focuses on "what's in it for me." Most people want "new challenges" in the next job. When too much focus is on the challenge, it takes away from what you bring to the job. The bottom line to the interview process is "What can you bring to this company from your past experiences and successes?"

The Weakest Answer

[**B**] This answer has all the indicators of a person who suffered from burnout and took any job just to survive. The interviewer might have reason to be concerned that this will happen again. It is best not to talk about the negatives of any job. Put the focus on the experience and skills you can bring to the new position: "I can bring added value to the job because of my past experience working in fast-paced environments."

RATE YOURSELF

If you chose answer [**A**], give yourself 5 points.

If you chose answer [**C**], give yourself 3 points.

If you chose answer [**B**], give yourself 0 points.

INTERVIEWER'S QUESTION

[7] "Tell me about a time when you had to overcome obstacles to get your job done."

Select the strongest answer.

[A] When I was a project manager for an entertainment company, I had to co-ordinate the video presentation for a very important meeting with an extremely tight deadline. The problem was that not all the film arrived. The first thing I did was get in touch with the other branches to see if anyone else had copies of the film. I was able to find everything I needed and have it shipped overnight. I stayed until three in the morning to get the project done, but it was quality work and was completed on time. My boss gave me extra points for getting through that one.

[B] I have to work around obstacles all the time. It's the nature of the job of managing projects. One day I have to work around money issues; the next day it's schedules and deadlines. Of course, I always have people problems to contend with. Every day I plan my day, and then, right when I am getting ahead, some problem occurs. Fortunately, I am known for my problem-solving ability.

[C] I have had many times in my jobs when I have had to put in extra time to solve some problem or obstacle that came up. One thing I always try to do is to think logically and stay focused. I usually can work through anything that comes my way. I have had times when a whole project depended on me to get it out the door on time. I came through with flying colors. My boss is sometimes amazed at what I can accomplish.

ANSWERS

The Strongest Answer

[**A**] This is the only answer of the three that addresses the question asked. The question begins, "Tell me about a time." Whenever you are asked about "a time," the interviewer is looking for a specific example. This answer shows that you handled the crisis, tells how you did it, and gives the result of your efforts.

The Mediocre Answer

[**C**] This is not a bad answer, but it doesn't answer the question that was asked. It is a very general answer and needs to be more specific. A lot of good qualities can be heard in this answer, but there is no specific example. Anyone can say he or she stays cool under pressure, but the interviewer is looking for an example of when you actually did that.

The Weakest Answer

[**B**] This answer is very general and does not provide an example of "a time when" you had to overcome an obstacle. It would be a much stronger answer if it included specific details of how and when you solved a problem. The tone of this answer could also be a problem. An interviewer might read between the lines and pick up on the idea that you are burned out on this work.

RATE YOURSELF

If you chose answer [**A**], give yourself 5 points.

If you chose answer [**C**], give yourself 3 points.

If you chose answer [**B**], give yourself 0 points.

INTERVIEWER'S QUESTION

[8] "Give me an example of a marketing strategy you've used."

Select the strongest answer.

[A] This was at my last company when I was a new account manager. The company made a special offer to customers, and it wasn't going well. The program had been running in the red for over a year. We did a lot of analysis, and we found out some information about the customer base—we discovered that we were targeting the wrong offer to the wrong consumer. When this happens, we have to work hard to get the customer to try our product again. This time we offered a better program with more cost savings. Because of the economy, we realized that people were being thrifty with their purchases, and we hadn't taken that factor into consideration when the product was launched. We were able to turn the situation around in the end.

[B] When I was the account manager in my last position, I was given a program that had been operating in the red for over a year. The program was one in which my company offered the customer a higher quality of merchandise and more points for buying. As it turned out, the problem was that we were targeting the wrong customer base. When the customers clicked on the website and saw such pricey merchandise, they were dropping out of the program rather than buying more. It was a very challenging situation for me, but I was able to turn it around quickly.

[C] I came into a situation as the account manager of a program that had been operating in the red for over a year. It was my role to turn the situation around as fast as possible. The first thing I did was to identify the issues and problems quickly. I began by looking at the profit and loss statements. Once I got the numbers, I discovered that a program that offered a higher-quality product to consumers was not being accepted mainly because of the economy. I was able to rapidly put in place a new program that offered customers cost savings instead. By focusing more on what the customer needed and the financial picture, I was able to turn the situation around in a short time. Needless to say, management was extremely happy with my solving the problem.

ANSWERS

The Strongest Answer

[**C**] This is the strongest answer of the three scenarios because it is very specific and detailed. The story follows the format of a beginning (what the problem was), the action (what you did), and the conclusion (what the outcome was). The problem is well defined, and the presentation is balanced. The answer demonstrates analysis and quick action to change a situation. You were successful in solving a problem and have given a good example of how you work in a negative situation.

The Mediocre Answer

[**B**] This is not the strongest answer because the emphasis is on the problem, with very little action or information about what you did. What action did you take? This story is too heavy on the situation and too light on the action, with only a brief mention of the result. Stories should be balanced, with the action having the most detail.

The Weakest Answer

[**A**] This answer is the weakest because it is a "we" story rather than an "I" story. Read it again and you will find that there are seven *wes* and one *I*. It is difficult for the interviewer to get a sense of your work if you don't talk about what your role was and what you did.

RATE YOURSELF

If you chose answer [**C**], give yourself 5 points.

If you chose answer [**B**], give yourself 3 points.

If you chose answer [**A**], give yourself 0 points.

INTERVIEWER'S QUESTION

[9] "Tell me about a time when you coordinated a project or event."

Select the strongest answer.

[A] I led a project to roll out a new product. A new exclusive package was being marketed for a specific store. One of the important factors was working closely with the finance department on a financial analysis. The challenge was to accomplish our goal within budget and still meet the customer's needs. We did primary and secondary research in order to do a competitive analysis of similar products. We were able to present the conclusions and recommendations successfully to top-level management with positive results.

[B] At a previous job, I led the rollout of a new product for an exclusive package to be featured in a major retail store. The first thing I did was to open channels of communication by meeting with the members of my team, letting them know as much detail about the project as I could. Next, I collaborated closely with all the other departments involved in the project. Through team effort, I was able to get primary and secondary research for the new product against the competition. We presented our results and recommendations to upper-level management for final approval and got strong commendations for our work as a team.

[C] I've been the lead on several new product rollouts. I always make sure that my team is informed. I also make sure that I am working collaboratively with the other departments, such as finance and the departments that are responsible for the supply chain. When I work on these types of projects, it is very important to me that we are on schedule and that all deadlines are met. My team is very responsive to my direction because the members know I deliver results. My main rule when coordinating a project is to keep the lines of communication open.

ANSWERS

The Strongest Answer

[**B**] This is the strongest answer because of the specifics given in answering the question. This answer goes through the steps to complete the process and shows how you work with others. Strong leadership and coordination skills are demonstrated clearly. Note that even though this was a team effort, you were able to demonstrate your role and use the word *I*.

The Mediocre Answer

[**A**] This is not as strong an answer as [**B**] because it does not answer the question and it focuses primarily on the problem. This answer gives very little detail about the steps taken. When you focus too heavily on the project or situation, you tend to stray from the subject and end up missing the opportunity to tell what you did and the successes you have had—and can have again.

The Weakest Answer

[**C**] This is the weakest answer because it roughly explains how you coordinated a project. All the right skills are present, but you don't bring up specific examples of how you achieved results. The fatal flaw in this answer is that it does not mention the results or the outcome at all. The success of the story will depend on your ability to show the problem, the action, and the result. What is a story without an ending?

RATE YOURSELF

If you chose answer [**B**], give yourself 5 points.

If you chose answer [**A**], give yourself 3 points.

If you chose answer [**C**], give yourself 0 points.

INTERVIEWER'S QUESTION

[10] "Give me an example of taking care of business day to day but also thinking long range."

Select the strongest answer.

[A] I am a project manager who keeps an eye on what's going on in the general market. Sometimes I have to respond quickly to get the market share, particularly in a tight economy. I usually spend a great deal of time working on the budget, attempting to maximize leverage. I've been known to take risks such as purchasing expensive advertising to get the word out. I am willing to do whatever it takes to compete in the market and feel that in the long run this will pay off. I've had experience leading some very successful campaigns even when market conditions weren't in our favor.

[B] Customer retention was a big challenge in my last company, where I was in charge of a marketing rollout. I worked with my staff and members of other relevant departments to strategize ways to retain first and build second. Teams interviewed customers, and the data collected were given to the marketing department for analysis. We obtained feedback from our customers stating that they wanted to be asked first or wanted information on request only. They didn't like our current telemarketing campaign and were annoyed because they were receiving information they didn't want or need. By working collaboratively and involving other departments, I was able to see a day-to-day problem with an impact on the bigger picture.

[C] I believe in the team approach where we work together to accomplish the end result. In my company we work as one entity when we have a big project. Whenever we have an event we all keep an eye on the bottom line, namely the deadline. Although we take care of planning and organizing, we still feel challenged working together to make things run smoothly while thinking of the bigger picture. This is an area I feel that I excel at, bringing like-minded people together to do the day-to-day job tasks while thinking longer term.

ANSWERS

The Strongest Answer

[**B**] This is the strongest answer. It is succinct and to the point. It talks about a specific problem and mentions the solution. The example indicates your ability to see the day-to-day issues while keeping an eye on the future and doing that by working with teams and departments across functions to get the maximum impact.

The Mediocre Answer

[**C**] This is a weaker answer than it could be because of its overuse of the pronoun *we*. If you count, you can find seven *we*s, which is too many to include if you want to show what your role was in this process. Even though you were working with teams and other departments, it is important that the interviewer hear your action in the activities.

The Weakest Answer

[**A**] This is not a strong answer because it does not focus on the question directly. The answer could be strengthened by adding an example of one of those "successful campaigns" you talk about.

RATE YOURSELF

If you chose answer [**B**], give yourself 5 points.

If you chose answer [**C**], give yourself 3 points.

If you chose answer [**A**], give yourself 0 points.

Interview IQ Scorecard: What's Your Interview IQ Score?

Insert your score for each question in the blank following it. Then calculate your total score for the 10 questions.

Management and Executive Questions

1. "Let's begin by your telling me about yourself." _____

2. "Give me a specific example of a time when you took the initiative." _____

3. "Describe your leadership or management style." _____

4. "Describe a time when you had to make an unpopular decision." _____

5. "Tell me about a time when you had to link long-range visions and strategies to day-to-day work." _____

6. "In what ways has your current or last job prepared you to take on more responsibility?" _____

7. "Tell me about a time when you had to overcome obstacles to get your job done." _____

8. "Give me an example of a marketing strategy you've used." _____

9. "Tell me about a time when you coordinated a project or event." _____

10. "Give me an example of taking care of business day to day but also thinking long range." _____

PART IV

Career Changers and Reentry

Changing careers or reentering the workforce can feel very intimidating to someone who is facing a tough job market plus a tough sell. Employers are in the driver's seat with so many applicants to choose from, and this can put you in a position of feeling less qualified than others.

The first thing to do is to stop focusing on what you *don't have* and start focusing on what you *do have*. Reading through a job description and doing a "compare and contrast" exercise between what is needed in the new job and what you did in your former jobs will be one way to convince yourself that you have something to offer. Jobs are often more alike than they are different as far as skills required.

Another confidence builder will be to focus on your strengths by doing an inventory of your transferable skills: these are the skills that you can bring to any company. And sometimes it will be your *personal traits* that will make you unique. You will have to feel confident that you have something to offer and that you are not a beginner. You bring experience—that is either rusty or in a different field.

By taking the general quiz to see how you do overall, you can get a feeling for where you need some preparation and confidence building.

The Interview IQ Test below, with its focus on changing careers and reentering the workplace, is aimed at you and some of the difficult questions that could make you feel intimidated. If you think about it, everyone is a "beginner" in a new job. Every job is challenging from the first day. It's just when you are entering a new field, you will have more work to do in order to bring yourself up to speed. If you believe you are capable of doing that, then let the interviewer hear that in your answers.

The Interview IQ Test:
Career Changers and Reentry Questions

INTERVIEWER'S QUESTION

[1] "Let's begin with your telling me about yourself."

Select the strongest answer.

[A] I was born in Cincinnati. My mother was a nurse, and my father was a lawyer. I went to the local high school and then attended the state college and graduated with a major in English. I worked for four years at a high-tech company, where I was a customer service rep. Then I moved to a large company and worked there for two years as a help desk rep. I was at my last company for one year as a manager of customer service.

[B] I have a total of seven years in the customer service field. In my last job, I managed a team of 14 reps. I have excellent communication and interpersonal skills, and that allows me to work with a broad range of people at various levels. My background includes working in Fortune 500 companies as well as smaller companies. My strength is my ability to organize and coordinate projects, making sure deadlines are met.

[C] I'd be glad to. Would you like to know about my personal life or my professional life? What would you like me to focus on?

ANSWERS

The Strongest Answer

[**B**] This is the strongest answer because it presents a good summary of what you have to offer. The interviewer now knows how many years of experience you have, what types of companies you have worked for, and what you consider your strengths are relative to the job. The answer also provides a good blend of knowledge-based skills, transferable skills, and some personality traits. You are striving to give the interviewer a good snapshot of yourself.

The Mediocre Answer

[**A**] This answer is all right but is not as strong an answer as [**B**]. This is basically a "walk-through-the-résumé" type of answer: "I was born, attended college, and worked at . . ." It would benefit from more detail and specifics, such as the types of companies you worked for or some of your strengths and personal characteristics. The ideal answer contains a well-rounded, current picture of you.

The Weakest Answer

[**C**] This is a very common reply to this question but is a weak answer. It does not show any preparation or planning in regard to what the employer would be interested in knowing about you. Your reply to this question is your opportunity to lead the interview and start out by focusing on what you want the interviewer to know about you and your qualifications for the position.

RATE YOURSELF

If you chose answer [**B**], give yourself 5 points.

If you chose answer [**A**], give yourself 3 points.

If you chose answer [**C**], give yourself 0 points.

INTERVIEWER'S QUESTION

[2] "How would your current or last boss describe your job performance?"

Select the strongest answer.

[A] Unfortunately, my last boss and I had very different personalities, and sometimes this resulted in conflicts. I think he would tell you that I was above all a professional in all my dealings with customers, internal and external. He also would tell you that I was reliable and met all my deadlines.

[B] She would tell you that I was her "right-hand man." She would make the decisions, and I did the background and technical work. She relied on me to do all the calculations and data input on projects. I kept her on track when she was running behind schedule, and I jumped in when she needed a hand. She would tell you that I was still her friend even though it's been five years since we worked together.

[C] He would tell you that I have excellent skills working with all kinds of people. He nominated me for an in-service award for my excellent customer service work within the company. He treated me with respect and gave me the feedback I needed to learn and grow in my job. He also would tell you that I was very dependable and could be trusted with confidential information.

ANSWERS

The Strongest Answer

[**B**] This is the strongest answer because it gives a clear picture of the way you work with authority: supportive and responsible. This answer informs the interviewer about your technical skills and abilities as well as your flexibility and willingness. It also speaks of the relationship you built with your boss. Not all jobs end with personal relationships, but if you can quote your boss or mention something positive that a boss said in a performance review, it will strengthen your answer.

The Mediocre Answer

[**C**] This is an acceptable answer but is not as strong as answer [**B**] because it is not as specific. It points out good communication and people skills as well as your being dependable and meeting deadlines, which is good, but it would be better with an example. The fact that you were nominated for an award is definitely worth mentioning and would benefit from some specifics.

The Weakest Answer

[**A**] This is a weak answer. It's best to avoid talking about differences in a negative way. Although this answer does not really bad-mouth the employer, it points out that there was a problem. The interviewer's concern would be that you did not get along well with your bosses. The answer does have a positive slant because it talks about being professional and meeting deadlines. A good interviewer would probe further and find out the nature of the conflicts. It's best to offer additional information when asked for it, but you don't necessarily have to volunteer to talk about problems.

RATE YOURSELF

If you chose answer [**B**], give yourself 5 points.

If you chose answer [**C**], give yourself 3 points.

If you chose answer [**A**], give yourself 0 points.

INTERVIEWER'S QUESTION

[3] "What do you think are the key qualities for a support person?"

Select the strongest answer.

[A] I know from experience that communication is the most critical. A good support person deals with a number of executives and key customers and needs to be able to communicate with them as a professional. Communication skills are extremely important in planning social events and conferences. I know that communication skills are the key element in the success of a project. All my bosses have depended heavily on my communication skills to convey messages and explain sensitive situations when necessary.

[B] It really depends on the nature of the job and the responsibilities involved. I sometimes work with support groups and at other times with individual bosses. Whatever I do, I try to accommodate each person as well as I can. If I am working for an individual, I work as a "right-hand man." I have been able to support the people I have worked for by staying flexible and trying to satisfy the requirements presented to me.

[C] Some of the key skills necessary to be a good support person are being organized, having good communication skills, being flexible, being reliable, and being a team player. These particular skills are some of the skills I pride myself on having. I have excellent communication skills and respond well when asked to work on projects that are not a part of my job description. I respond quickly and never miss deadlines. My teammates would tell you that if I don't have something to do, I ask others if I can be of help.

ANSWERS

The Strongest Answer

[**C**] This is the strongest answer because it names the key qualities and then takes the opportunity to point out that you have them. By talking about your key skills, this answer becomes stronger, especially with the "teammate" endorsement. Never answer a question with a single-word answer. Always take the opportunity to give an example or at least expand on the answer.

The Mediocre Answer

[**A**] This is not a bad answer, but it focuses on only one quality—communication—instead of naming the key qualities, as specified in the question. The answer gives good examples of communication skills and the way you have used the skills in your past work. It would be stronger if you had answered the question as asked. Be sure you are listening to and answering the questions asked.

The Weakest Answer

[**B**] This is the weakest answer because it lacks the focus to convey what the key qualities are and whether you have them. By giving a "neutral" answer, you fail to make an impact. In this case, the question did not ask about "your" key qualities but about what you thought the key qualities were. It is all right to say that you have the qualities needed as long as you answer the question at the same time.

RATE YOURSELF

If you chose answer [**C**], give yourself 5 points.

If you chose answer [**A**], give yourself 3 points.

If you chose answer [**B**], give yourself 0 points.

INTERVIEWER'S QUESTION

[4] "I have a concern about your being overqualified for this position. Do you believe you're overqualified?"

Select the strongest answer.

[A] I can assure you that I always work hard and get my work done no matter what my title or my salary. My work is very important to me, and I want to make a difference. When you talk about being overqualified, I'm not sure what that means. If you think my salary is too high, I can assure you that the opportunity is far more important than the pay. I want this job, and if you choose me, I will prove I can do the job, bringing my experience and successes with me.

[B] From the first time I read the posting for this position, I knew that I could do the job, and do it well. I have extensive experience that will enhance the position as described, bringing new ideas and methods. I'm excited about the opportunity to do what I do well. I have a record of success in bringing in results and making things run more efficiently. From what we've been talking about today, I feel I could be the solution to your problem. I wouldn't call that overqualified. I'd call that a good deal.

[C] That would depend on your definition of overqualified. I have been in this industry a long time. I remember when we did things without computers. I have learned the hard way, not just from taking classes like these young kids do but through hard work and trial and error. I have a great work ethic, and anyone who has ever worked for me would tell you I'm a dedicated person who is very reliable. I always meet the deadlines and goals that I set for myself. I was taught that you earn your pay, not just collect it by showing up.

ANSWERS

The Strongest Answer

[**B**] This is the strongest answer because it sounds upbeat, confident, and persuasive. You can bring things to the job that this company needs. You can provide added value from your past experiences and successes. One of the concerns when someone is overqualified is that he or she won't stick around. That concern could be addressed in subsequent answers about short-term and long-term goals.

The Mediocre Answer

[**A**] The answer isn't bad; it just has a tone of desperation, almost like begging for the job. This should be a situation that is win-win for everyone: "Here's what I have to offer. What are you looking for?" One of the concerns about someone who has many years of experience is that the salary requirement will be too high. Nevertheless, it is best not to bring up this subject until the interviewer asks about it.

The Weakest Answer

[**C**] This answer sounds dusty and needs to be refreshed. When someone thinks you are overqualified, he or she may relate that to your years of experience. One of the things the interviewer may be concerned with is your ability to be *cutting edge*. When you talk about not having computers in the "good old days," interviewers begin to think their suspicions are correct. Vocabulary is very important in an interview; it could make the difference between success and failure.

RATE YOURSELF

If you chose answer [**B**], give yourself 5 points.

If you chose answer [**A**], give yourself 3 points.

If you chose answer [**C**], give yourself 0 points.

INTERVIEWER'S QUESTION

[5] "Why should we hire you?"

Select the strongest answer.

[A] I can do this job. I know I can. Because I am a quick learner, I have the ability to pick up things faster than most people. I am eager to learn and am currently taking classes to learn some of the computer programs I don't know. I can learn this job very fast and be useful almost immediately. I am looking for an opportunity to try something new.

[B] My strong people skills are what I can bring to this job and company. I can work easily with almost every person I've been in contact with. I have an ability to read people and treat them as individuals in a way that most people can't. My customers always ask for me personally because they know I will give them excellent service. When I saw this job posted on the Internet, I knew that this was "my" job.

[C] If you compare my qualifications with your requirements, you will see that I am almost a perfect match for this position. You are seeking someone with the years of experience and skills I have acquired in this industry, and in addition to that I have excellent writing skills. I have the ability to work with a wide variety of people at all levels. If you were to ask my former colleagues, they would tell you, "She is one of a kind. She keeps the morale up and the work flowing."

ANSWERS

The Strongest Answer

[**C**] This is the strongest answer. The best way to persuade the interviewer that you are the best person for the job is to present yourself as being as close a match to the requirements as possible. Let the interviewer know that you are a match by describing your skills, particularly in the specific areas required. If you have something additional to bring to the job, that could make a difference; it could even be the deciding factor in whether you get the offer. Quoting colleagues or bosses helps prove your point without your having to say so.

The Mediocre Answer

[**B**] This is not as strong an answer as answer [**C**], but it has the right tone. Consider stating one or two strong points that you have outside the job description: an "added value." This answer also shows the strong confidence you have in yourself and your ability to do the job.

The Weakest Answer

[**A**] This is the weakest answer because it has a desperate tone. It's a difficult sell when you do not have the requirements for the job. This answer does demonstrate an eager attitude and a proven ability to learn quickly, which is the right approach to take when you are lacking skills. Remember that the company is not in business to teach you new things but to get the work done. At the same time, companies usually look for people who are willing to grow and learn new things.

RATE YOURSELF

If you chose answer [**C**], give yourself 5 points.

If you chose answer [**B**], give yourself 3 points.

If you chose answer [**A**], give yourself 0 points.

INTERVIEWER'S QUESTION

[6] "Do you have any questions?"

Select the strongest answer.

[A] I would like to know about the bonus situation and how it is decided who will receive a bonus and who will not. I also would like to know more about payment of the premiums on healthcare insurance.

[B] You have been very thorough in your explanation of what the job entails. I don't have any further questions at this time. I'm sure I would have more questions once I started the job.

[C] One thing that has been talked about during the interview process is the "branding" of your product. Could you tell me what has worked to this point and what you would expect to see done differently?

ANSWERS

The Strongest Answer

[**C**] This is the strongest answer because it shows that you have been listening and are aware that one of your first projects will be to work on the "branding" issue. The bottom line of the interviewing process is "What can you do for us?" By asking what has worked and what has not, you demonstrate an ability to listen to the problem, and then you can address what is needed to solve the problem. By listening carefully what has been said, you will be able to ask questions that are of interest to "them."

The Mediocre Answer

[**A**] Depending on where you are in the interview process, this answer could be appropriate. This would not be a good question to ask in a first interview before any interest is shown. This answer or question on your part focuses on what you will get out of working for this company. You will need the information eventually; just wait until the appropriate time to bring it up, such as during a second interview or when it is clear that an offer is pending.

The Weakest Answer

[**B**] This is the most common reply used by candidates—"No, I don't have any questions"—and it is the wrong answer. It is very important that you ask questions to show your interest and let the interviewer know you have been listening. Some managers will ask an interviewer to keep track of the questions asked by the candidate to see where the interest lies. You should focus on what the company's problem is and what you are expected to do if you get the position.

RATE YOURSELF

If you chose answer [**C**], give yourself 5 points.

If you chose answer [**A**], give yourself 3 points.

If you chose answer [**B**], give yourself 0 points.

INTERVIEWER'S QUESTION

[7] "Why do you want to work here? What attracts you to this job?"

Select the strongest answer.

[A] I know I could do this job. When I read through the job description and compared it with what I have to offer, it looked like a perfect match for your position. You can see from my résumé that I have been at my company for three years, and I tend to get complacent when I have accomplished all my goals with nowhere to advance. I think that your job would fill all of my requirements and would be a job where I could grow and develop and be challenged.

[B] I've been searching for a company with the specific mission of helping people to get jobs. When I came across your position and began to research the company's goals and accomplishments, I knew that this is where I wanted to work. I want to make a difference and feel good about my job and my contribution to the company and to helping people. When I researched further using social networking, I found so many positive comments from employees, product users, and vendors. That really impressed me, and I set a goal to work for this company.

[C] I've been looking at job postings for a few months and your description was very detailed on what you were looking for. I liked that there were some of the same values and skills that I have to offer. It is very important to me to be able to relate to the product or services provided by the company I work for. Integrity is a big factor for me. I did some research and didn't find any comments that discouraged me from applying at your company. I also like the company's location, and my commute will be quite easy.

ANSWERS

The Strongest Answer

[**B**] This is the strongest answer because it focuses on the company and how you are interested in what it does and what it stands for. By focusing on the company and letting the interviewer know that you have "passion" about what it does, you will appear to be on the same wavelength as the company is. The interviewer is looking for enthusiastic people to become a part of the organization or team. Genuine "flattery" will let the interviewer know that you understand the product or the culture of the company and want to be a part of the team.

The Mediocre Answer

[**C**] This is a mediocre answer because the tone implies that you accidentally stumbled onto the job posting. Your answer is OK because you do say that you did some research and found the values and skills in line with what you have to offer. The statement "I did some research and didn't find any comments that discouraged me from applying at your company" would be a stronger statement by emphasizing the positive. A more positive way of saying the same thing is: "When I did some further research, all the comments I saw were very positive and made me want to work at this company." By saying statements in the positive you appear to be more upbeat.

The Weakest Answer

[**A**] This is the weakest answer because it focuses on your wants rather than on the specific job itself. There are also some "red flags" broadcast in this answer: "I tend to become complacent when I have accomplished all my goals." One of the concerns of the interviewer is about how long you will stick around. If you tend to get bored and need a challenge, that could be seen as an issue about how long you will be satisfied and stay in the position. While it's good to want to be challenged and to grow and develop, it is not wise to focus on that issue during the interview. The interviewer is looking for someone to come in and do the job right away.

RATE YOURSELF

If you chose answer [**B**], give yourself 5 points.

If you chose answer [**C**], give yourself 3 points.

If you chose answer [**A**], give yourself 0 points.

INTERVIEWER'S QUESTION

[8] "What is your greatest weakness?"

Select the strongest answer.

[A] I am always working on my ability to get along with difficult people. I think the biggest challenge of any job is trying to avoid conflict and get along with everyone. I consider myself to be an easygoing person. It's just that some people can take advantage of that fact, and that can cause problems.

[B] My people skills have been my strongest asset working in the customer service field. I do admit, however, that sometimes I am challenged to rise above what is going on and be objective about how I handle things with coworkers and customers. This is something I continually work on. In fact, I am currently reading a book that is a huge help in understanding the different personalities in the workplace and how to handle them.

[C] My real weakness is that I am a perfectionist. I like to do things right. I am a stickler for dotting my *i*'s and crossing my *t*'s. I get really frustrated when other people's lack of caring makes my work suffer. We had a lot of people with indifferent attitudes at my last company, and that's one of the reasons I am seeking a new job in a new company.

ANSWERS

The Strongest Answer

[**B**] This is the strongest answer because it starts out on a positive note with a strength. It then moves into negative territory with a weakness and concludes with a positive—what you are doing to work on your weakness. This is a good formula for answering this dreaded question. Focus on something that you are working on to improve yourself and explain what you are doing to change. The answer formula is positive statement—negative problem—positive statement.

The Mediocre Answer

[**A**] This is an OK answer, but it could raise some red flags for the interviewer. Do you have problems getting along with people? By *avoiding* problems are you being passive? The passive behavior of putting up with something can turn into aggressive behavior if pushed to its limit. It is best to stay away from problems that could impact your performance in a negative way.

The Weakest Answer

[**C**] This answer tries to overcome the weakness by stating a strong trait—being a perfectionist. The problem is that any trait taken to extreme can become a negative. While it is good to want to do things *right*, there is a point when perfectionism in the workplace can go too far. Judging others' work ethic against your own and complaining about coworkers in an interview is not a good idea. This answer would be stronger if you ended on a positive note—what you are doing to deal with your frustration working with others who don't have the same work ethic.

RATE YOURSELF

If you chose answer [**B**], give yourself 5 points.

If you chose answer [**A**], give yourself 3 points.

If you chose answer [**C**], give yourself 0 points.

INTERVIEWER'S QUESTION

[9] "Tell me about a time when you took initiative over something that you saw needed to be done."

Select the strongest answer.

[A] As an officer in the military, I had many occasions to initiate action. There was one time when I had to make a quick decision that made the difference between whether or not lives were saved. A signal that should have been given was not, and as a result, men were being shot at that shouldn't have been. By making an independent decision, I called a cease-fire. I was able to stop the action and keep my troops from being seriously injured or killed that day.

[B] I am a person who tries to plan ahead, and so I usually have a planned schedule for every step of a project. There was a time when my plan started to come undone due to unforeseen happenings. What I did was to stop all activities until I could regroup. If I had let things progress, I could see that the ending was not going to have the results we needed to finish the project. As it turned out, we did complete the project, and my plan was completed as I had hoped it would be.

[C] As a project manager for my last company, I could see a need for a template to guide team members through projects. I worked on a prototype and presented it to my manager. He liked the idea and encouraged me to follow up and develop it. I made some changes based on my team's suggestions. When I gave the final guide to the members of my team, they were delighted to have a format to assist them in organizing their tasks. My boss presented the guide to management, and it is now used companywide. I received an award for initiating a more efficient process that will save time and ultimately money.

ANSWERS

The Strongest Answer

[**C**] This is the strongest answer on many fronts. It gives a specific example of a time when you actually took initiative. By allowing the interviewer to see the action taken to complete the task, he or she gets a clear picture of the way you handle situations. The ending of this example is especially impressive because not only were you rewarded, but your actions determined a process that saved time and money. The interviewer will want to hear more to find out other times when you had money-saving ideas and how you dealt with them.

The Mediocre Answer

[**A**] This is a mediocre answer not because it has weak content but because it leaves unanswered questions. There is no doubt that there was a quick decision and that initiative was taken, but what happened in between is somewhat of a mystery. Quick thinking and good judgment are excellent transferable skills, but you will need to give more details about what happened. More emphasis is needed on what the decision-making process entailed and what was at risk with the judgment.

The Weakest Answer

[**B**] This answer really misses the mark as far as initiating an action. In fact, this answer is so vague that it is difficult to see what you were trying to accomplish except to follow a plan. The answer gives very little information other than sharing that you are a planner and like to have things follow a plan. The answer does have a successful ending, indicating that your actions of stopping and regrouping were the right things to do.

RATE YOURSELF

If you chose answer [**C**], give yourself 5 points.

If you chose answer [**A**], give yourself 3 points.

If you chose answer [**B**], give yourself 0 points.

INTERVIEWER'S QUESTION

[10] "What salary are you (or were you) making at your job?"

Select the strongest answer.

[A] It would be very difficult for me to compare my last salary with what I would expect to earn at this position for various reasons—primarily because I don't have enough information about your whole package. I'm sure we can discuss this subject and your entire package before an offer is made.

[B] That would be like comparing two jobs that are entirely different in responsibilities and in the base and bonus structure. I would be more interested in hearing what the package you offer is, before I compare the two jobs. I hope we can postpone this subject until we both have more information to discuss salary and benefit comparisons.

[C] I had an unusual situation at my last job where I took less salary to own a share of the company. I also had a bonus structure that I was receiving. I would have to look at the entire package that you offer before comparing the two jobs or salaries.

ANSWERS

The Strongest Answer

[**B**] This is the strongest answer of the three. It sounds in control and has the correct attitude about salary comparisons. It is very difficult to compare one job and the benefits of that job with another job that may have different responsibilities and accountability. If you can postpone the salary discussion until a later time when you have more information, it would be in your interest to do that.

The Mediocre Answer

[**A**] This answer is OK but is not as confident sounding as [**B**]. The answer postpones the discussion until you have more information. If the interviewer pushes back and wants to know a number, you can try to talk in *ranges*, for example, $40,000 to $50,000. The problem with this question is that compensation is a package and not a stand-alone number. Everything has a price tag, from a vacation to a 401(k) matching plan, and therefore impacts the final number.

The Weakest Answer

[**C**] This answer is the weakest but is really not a bad answer. Once again, it postpones the discussion, which is the right thing to do—depending on where you are in the process. Because there were so many different circumstances that determined your last salary, it might cause the interviewer to think that you may not *settle* for what the job pays. It is best to keep the conversation general, without all the details if possible.

RATE YOURSELF

If you chose answer [**B**], give yourself 5 points.

If you chose answer [**A**], give yourself 3 points.

If you chose answer [**C**], give yourself 0 points.

Interview IQ Scorecard:
What's Your Interview IQ Score?

Insert your score for each question in the blank following it. Then calculate your total score for the 10 questions.

Career Changers and Reentry Questions

1. "Let's begin with your telling me about yourself." _____

2. "How would your current or last boss describe your job performance?" _____

3. "What do you think are the key qualities for a support person?" _____

4. "I have a concern about your being overqualified for this position. Do you believe you're overqualified?" _____

5. "Why should we hire you?" _____

6. "Do you have any questions?" _____

7. "In what ways has your current or last job prepared you to take on more responsibility?" _____

8. "What is your greatest weakness?" _____

9. "Tell me about a time when you took initiative over something that you saw needed to be done." _____

10. "What salary are you (or were you) making at your job?" _____

PART V

Students and New Graduates

Anytime you're trying to do something new, you usually don't have as much confidence as someone who has a great deal of experience to draw from. But when it comes to interviewing for a job, you do have resources to call on that you may not realize. For example, you have experiences and stories from your education, classes you took, part-time work you've done, volunteer work you've been doing, and internships and externships you've completed. Maybe you've served on a committee, been an officer for your fraternity or sorority, or led a group project; or maybe there's something interesting about your hobbies or your personal life experiences. These topics will become the basis for the stories you will relate to the interviewer when you are asked certain questions.

As in the other quizzes in the book, this quiz will ask you to identify the strongest answer to the question.

Note that this section is not limited to students and new grads alone. The answers are more in line with student interview questions and responses, but they are not limited in scope. And in the same spirit, if you are a student or a new graduate, you are encouraged to take the general and behavioral sections of the Interview IQ Test, found in Part 1, as well.

The Interview IQ Test:
Students and New Graduates Questions

INTERVIEWER'S QUESTION

[1] "Did you have any problems getting here this morning?"

Select the strongest answer.

[A] No. I used Google maps. No problem.

[B] I did take a couple of wrong turns, and the traffic was pretty bad, but I had planned ahead and allowed extra time so I was OK. This is really a nice facility in a good location.

[C] I am one of those people that leave nothing to chance. I mapped out my route last night and then listened to the radio in the car to keep abreast of traffic. I actually had time to grab a quick cup of coffee.

ANSWERS

The Strongest Answer

[**C**] This is the strongest answer because it shows planning and forethought. Employers seek candidates who are resourceful and think ahead. Another important key factor is adaptability. This answer shows that if necessary, an alternative route would have been taken depending on traffic. Obviously, if you are not a planner, this answer wouldn't work for you—but get the idea of talking a bit more about your decision-making process.

The Mediocre Answer

[**B**] This is an OK answer but does not show the skills that answer [**C**] shows. We are always revealing information about ourselves and giving indications about whether we are observant. If appropriate, it is nice to give a compliment about an office or location or building. Flattery and compliments can go a long way.

The Weakest Answer

[**A**] This is a very weak answer. It just gives the "facts." While it speaks to new technology, and that's good, it is a flat answer. The idea of the interview is to engage with the interviewer and make a connection. It is often difficult for new grads and students to make small talk with strangers. It would be a good idea for you to practice making small talk with other people that you are comfortable talking with. Staying current and reading up on news events, trends, and fads are good ways to help you talk to almost anyone once you find a common interest.

RATE YOURSELF

If you chose answer [**C**], give yourself 5 points.

If you chose answer [**B**], give yourself 3 points.

If you chose answer [**A**], give yourself 0 points.

INTERVIEWER'S QUESTION

[2] "Tell me about yourself."

Select the strongest answer.

[A] To begin, I am in the process of finishing up my BA in finance, which I will complete in December. I have worked with computers since I was young and am able to take a problem and work through a solution using a combination of technology and analytical thinking. I have a high work ethic, and you could even call me "hungry" when it comes to work. I will do whatever it takes to get the job done—including staying up until 5 and 6 a.m.

[B] Overall, I think I am very well rounded. I have many interests, including music, film, sports, current events, and politics. I have played sports in high school and college and consider myself to be a team player. I think something that makes me unique as a candidate is that I am very entrepreneurial. I've been investing in the stock market since I was 15 and started my own businesses in high school.

[C] I graduated last year with a degree in science. I have maintained a 4.0 in my major and have been on the dean's list–first honors three times. I know several computer programs and languages, including SQL, Java, and Visual Basic; and I have worked part-time while going to school as a tutor to students during the school year. Some of my projects while in college were computing analytical and conceptual problems using Excel and forecasting data with SPSS for applied statistical methods.

ANSWERS

The Strongest Answer

[**A**] This answer is the strongest of the three. It answers the question "Tell me about yourself" and offers a broad picture of you as a person. It includes skills and traits and, the hope is, entices the interviewer to want to know more. It is a good point to talk about your work ethic and your attitude toward hard work.

The Mediocre Answer

[**C**] This answer offers a great deal of information about you and your education but is basically the answer to the question "Walk me through your résumé." You may be asked that question in an interview, but it is not the same answer you would provide when asked "Tell me about yourself." This answer focuses primarily on your knowledge-based skills with very little information about your traits or personal qualities. The strongest answer offers a more comprehensive picture of who you are as a person as well as a student.

The Weakest Answer

[**B**] For the most part, this answer is very general, which makes it a weak answer. Failing to give specifics, you are betting on the fact that your résumé was not only read but studied. Oftentimes an interviewer will skim the résumé, and so it is a good idea to offer some background information. There are some interesting facts in this answer, but it needs more structure and detail.

RATE YOURSELF

If you chose answer [**A**], give yourself 5 points.

If you chose answer [**C**], give yourself 3 points.

If you chose answer [**B**], give yourself 0 points.

INTERVIEWER'S QUESTION

[3] "Why do you want to work for this company?"

Select the strongest answer.

[A] I am very anxious to start my career. I know that your company is among the best in the industry, and I think it would be a good start for my career—to work for the best. I want to work for a company that has a good reputation and good benefits. I also know that your company's compensation is fair, and in fact generous. I know this is a place where I can grow and develop as a stepping-stone to my career.

[B] When I started my education, I was very thorough in researching the field that I wanted to work in and found your company and two others that were leaders in the industry. At that time, I started to follow the stocks, profits, and growth of the companies. Your company has been the front-runner consistently. I have also done research on your founders and the company mission statement and philosophy, and I like what I see. This is the company I want to work for long term to build a solid foundation in this industry.

[C] I have been applying to the companies that have come on campus to interview. I think this is a great opportunity to find out about these companies and whether I would want to work there. I know your company is a first choice of many students, and I like that. I am looking for a company where I can grow and develop and utilize my education and skills.

ANSWERS

The Strongest Answer

[**B**] This is the strongest answer because it shows that there is a history of interest in the company as well as an extensive knowledge of the company's success and growth. Companies—the interviewers and hiring managers—have "ego." They are looking for passion and enthusiasm from candidates who want to work at their company. It is very flattering to all concerned if you have done your research and want to work at their company.

The Mediocre Answer

[**A**] This answer is more about you and what you will get out of the company than it is about wanting to work there. It is fine to want things from a company, but in the answer to this question, the interviewer more likely wants to know why you chose to interview there and what you expect. Is there a real interest, or is it a means to an end?

The Weakest Answer

[**C**] The reason you state about why you want to work there is very superficial It sounds like you are going for the "popular" company rather than wanting to work there because of the mission statement or values of the company. It also doesn't sound like you did any research other than talk to your fellow students.

RATE YOURSELF

If you chose answer [**B**], give yourself 5 points.

If you chose answer [**A**], give yourself 3 points.

If you chose answer [**C**], give yourself 0 points.

INTERVIEWER'S QUESTION

[4] "What do you think that you can bring to this position?"

Select the strongest answer.

[A] My strength is my ability to deal with people. This has a lot to do with the fact that I am a good listener and that I am good at reading people. I have worked since I was 14 years old, and I have worked with a huge diversity of people and always been able to adapt and get along by adjusting my style and vocabulary to meet the person's level.

[B] I have a very high work ethic and am known for being someone who is always looking for more work to do. I think my coworkers would describe me as a "nice guy," one who has a lot of respect for others. I have a lot of energy and know how to channel that energy to get things done—on time. I am extremely organized and efficient with time management.

[C] I would say my analytical problem solving. My engineering education and internships have taught me the problem-solving process of planning, trouble-shooting, and researching. I value projects that are done collaboratively, which allows me to be involved in far more sophisticated procedures working with other people and their ideas. I have the ability to get along with almost anyone.

ANSWERS

The Strongest Answer

[**C**] This is the strongest of the three answers because it focuses on knowledge-based traits—education and training. These are the traits that will satisfy the requirements of the job. Knowledge-based traits should not be the *only* skills or traits you let the interviewer know that you can bring to the job, but they are probably the most important to getting the job done—depending on the job.

The Mediocre Answer

[**A**] This is not a bad answer but is not as strong as [**C**]. This answer focuses on your transferable skills, which are definitely important. Depending on the job that you are going for, they could be the most important skills needed to get the job done. Communication and interpersonal skills are desirable in almost any job. If you combine this answer with answer [**B**], you would have a very strong answer that talks about your knowledge-based skills as well as your transferable skills and personal traits.

The Weakest Answer

[**B**] This is the weakest answer because it is not very impressive when it comes to competing with other candidates who will talk about education and communication skills. Being a "nice guy" usually doesn't impress in the interview. High energy and a good attitude are important but may not be enough to compete with other candidates who have more to offer in the other areas. The answer needs some "muscle" to be the best answer.

RATE YOURSELF

If you chose answer [**C**], give yourself 5 points.

If you chose answer [**A**], give yourself 3 points.

If you chose answer [**B**], give yourself 0 points.

INTERVIEWER'S QUESTION

[5] "Tell me about a time when you had to deal with a difficult person."

Select the strongest answer.

[A] When I was a graduate student, I was required to present research to the entire department. The department chair didn't like my mentor and took every opportunity to criticize my work to get back at him through me. I became so frustrated that I finally had a straight talk with the department chair, letting him know that I was being squeezed in a battle that had nothing to do with me. I think I surprised him by coming in and confronting him.

[B] One of the players on my rugby team was very outspoken and sometimes picked on other players who weren't as strong as he was. I could see that the team was starting to be affected by this bullying. I decided to do something about it. I approached the bully and asked him if I could talk to him. He didn't want to talk, but I convinced him that what I had to say was important. We didn't really have a discussion—more like a shouting match—but at the end I think I got my point across. He didn't stop his bullying behavior completely after that, but he did improve.

[C] While I was in college, I worked weekends as a referee for a soccer association, which was not an easy job. One day in particular, I had a coach who was giving me a bad time and yelling profanities at me across the field. What I did to control this situation was to walk over to the sideline where the disruptive coach was. He said how horrible the calls were. I told him that he could not be yelling the obscenities from the sideline and that he must control himself better or I would eject him from the game. I told him this is your last warning and if I need to speak to you again during this game, you will be ejected. The coach got very quiet. I then said thank you and blew the whistle to restart play, and the rest of the game went without incident.

ANSWERS

The Strongest Answer

[**C**] This is the strongest answer because it is a complete story about a time when you dealt with a difficult person. The story has a beginning—a setting and your role. The story has an action part—"What I did to control this situation was . . ." And the story has an ending—there were no more incidents after you spoke with authority.

The Mediocre Answer

[**B**] This is an OK story but doesn't have the depth that answer [**C**] has. What makes a story stronger is to "show"—not just "tell." More detail about what was said in the "shouting match" would have given the interviewer more information about how you handle yourself in tough situations.

The Weakest Answer

[**A**] This is the weakest answer because it does not have the correct structure of a story and leaves off the ending completely. The answer starts out on the right track but falls apart after that. It is important that you give a complete story when you answer a behavioral question.

RATE YOURSELF

If you chose answer [**C**], give yourself 5 points.

If you chose answer [**B**], give yourself 3 points.

If you chose answer [**A**], give yourself 0 points.

INTERVIEWER'S QUESTION

[6] "Tell me about the biggest project that you were involved in—in school or in your personal life."

Select the strongest answer.

[A] This was a group project that consisted of five people and made up 30 percent of our final grade for a public speaking class. The group named me the leader of the project, and to get going, I had the group pick our topic and come up with a general idea of the presentation. I talked to all the group members to find their strengths and weaknesses. According to their different skill sets, I divided up the job assignments. I scheduled weekly meetings and met numerous times with group members to help them with a problem or to critique their work. The result was that the group received the highest grade in the class. My professor stated that our group project was one of the best presentations she had seen in her class and that everyone in my group rated my work as "A" material.

[B] This example comes from my personal life as an active leader of a fraternity I belong to. Once a year we have a fund-raiser to raise money for children with cancer. It is a long-standing tradition in the house and raises over six figures every year. The challenge this year was the tight economy and the fact that contributions overall were down. We had several meetings to discuss how to overcome this obstacle and decided to do something different in our approach to our usual event. Instead of just having a regular big party, we decided that a theme would help make it more fun and festive. We came up with a 1980s theme, and everyone was encouraged to dress of that era. It turned out to be a great party and a huge success. We were able to raise more than 25 percent more money over the two previous years.

[C] I have been involved in a number of projects both in school and in my personal life. In fact, people look to me whenever there is a project to be organized. My cousin asked me to coordinate her wedding last year, and that was probably one of the biggest and most challenging projects that I have ever been involved in. I am great with details and use technology to track dates, times, names, and all those details you need to keep straight when you plan an event. One thing I liked about this job when I saw the description was that there is a great deal of planning and organizing.

ANSWERS

The Strongest Answer

[**A**] This is the strongest answer because it is a complete answer to the question. When giving this answer in an interview, the story would be longer with more detail about the planning and organizing and the way you kept on track with your own work while helping others. There are many skills that can be gleaned from this story—leadership, planning, organizing, assessment of people, ability to adapt to and work with a variety of people. When you answer a question, the interviewer is hearing more than just what you are saying—he or she is seeing a pattern of behavior and attitude.

The Mediocre Answer

[**B**] This is a great story, but where are you in the story? When you tell a story that is not about your actions, it is an entertaining story that gives the interviewer no new information about you other than that you were a part of a group project. In order to make this a stronger story, you will need to add a lot more detail about the planning and organizing of the event—but most of all detail about what you did to make the project a success. The interviewer is trying to get a picture of you and what you can do and bring to the job.

The Weakest Answer

[**C**] This is obviously the weakest answer because it doesn't answer the question or tell a story. If the answer had focused on the planning and organizing of the cousin's wedding, it could have been a strong answer. It isn't the topic of the story as much as it is the details of what your role was and what you did that makes a story stronger. This answer shows many good traits and skills but does not get specific.

RATE YOURSELF

If you chose answer [**A**], give yourself 5 points.

If you chose answer [**B**], give yourself 3 points.

If you chose answer [**C**], give yourself 0 points.

INTERVIEWER'S QUESTION

[7] "Tell about a time when you had many projects with the same deadline and how you handled the situation."

Select the strongest answer.

[A] As a student, I have had to juggle projects and deadlines on a continual basis. I am fortunate that I didn't have to work while attending school. I had a scholarship, and my parents were able to pay the rest of my expenses. But that didn't mean it was an easy ride. I have applied myself the whole time I have been in college. I've been able to maintain a high GPA and have participated in extra-curricular activities in sports and social events. I am very organized about my projects and have never missed a deadline.

[B] Because I work part-time and carry a full load each semester, I am con-stantly trying to balance between my life and my studies. I did have a really tight situation when I had four classes one semester and each class required a lengthy term paper. I had many nights with just a few hours of sleep and have to admit to skipping one class to write a paper for another. I learned to balance and survive and get good grades to boot.

[C] My last semester last year was my "waterloo." I was working 30 hours a week and taking 16 units and playing on a softball team. I knew from the beginning of the semester that I was going to have to be very organized to survive. What I did was put together a spreadsheet and designate blocks of time for different activi-ties and deadlines for each project or activity. I was able to program myself to the time requirements and to keep up. One of the biggest challenges was doing things like eating and sleeping—but I also tried to allow time to do those activi-ties and relax once in a while. If I hadn't planned my time, I know I would have never accomplished what I did.

ANSWERS

The Strongest Answer

[**C**] This is the strongest answer because of the details of how you planned and organized your time and were able to survive in a tough situation. Many job descriptions will say "Fast-paced environment" or "Deadline driven," and you will have to demonstrate your ability to handle stress. The question asks how you handled the situation, and this is a good answer to the question.

The Mediocre Answer

[**B**] This had all the makings of a strong answer, but it didn't take it far enough. The story doesn't have enough details. How did you manage to write all those papers? This is probably not a good place to talk about missing class to write a paper. The answer would suggest you do whatever it takes to get the job done— but also take some shortcuts on the way.

The Weakest Answer

[**A**] The answer says all the right things but doesn't get specific. In fact, it goes off the track a few times talking about scholarships and parents. When you talk about your personal finances during an interview you are giving information that is probably not relevant to the job. Remember to listen to the question asked and answer with comments that the interviewer will find interesting and applicable to the question.

RATE YOURSELF

If you chose answer [**C**], give yourself 5 points.

If you chose answer [**B**], give yourself 3 points.

If you chose answer [**A**], give yourself 0 points.

INTERVIEWER'S QUESTION

[8] "Do you have any questions?"

Select the strongest answer.

[A] Yes, I'd like to know more about your training programs. I've heard from friends that you have a program for entry-level people to work at a job for six months and then rotate to another location or department. I am very interested in training and learning opportunities. Would I be eligible to apply for this program?

[B] How long have you been with the company? And what do you like about working here?

[C] From what I've heard today and the questions you have asked, it sounds like this job is somewhat flexible about where I would be working. You mentioned earlier that there was a program where I might be changing positions every 6 to 12 months for a couple of years. This is really something I would like to pursue, as I feel it would be a benefit and opportunity to learn more about the different functions within the company. Can you tell me a bit more about the program and what it would take to qualify?

ANSWERS

The Strongest Answer

[**C**] This is the strongest answer for a couple of reasons. First, it is important to ask questions. The interviewer is waiting to hear what you ask about. If you have been listening, you will pick up on certain information that you can use to ask an intelligent question. Second, it shows the interviewer that you have been listening and not just waiting for the next question to be asked.

The Mediocre Answer

[**A**] This answer basically asks the same question as answer [**C**] but sounds more self-serving. Sometimes it's the tone or the way you ask a question that makes a difference. Before you start asking about how you apply to a program, you should make sure you will be receiving an offer. You want to sound interested in the company and how its program will benefit you but also in how this opportunity will make you a more valuable employee in the long run.

The Weakest Answer

[**B**] Do not just ask questions for the sake of asking questions. Some books will tell you to "interview" the interviewer, but when you turn the tables, you may not get positive results. Some interviewers may not like being asked personal questions—and some may like it—it depends on the situation and the interviewer. This would be a good question to ask if you were making informal conversation with the interviewer at an interview lunch or dinner.

RATE YOURSELF

If you chose answer [**C**], give yourself 5 points.

If you chose answer [**A**], give yourself 3 points.

If you chose answer [**B**], give yourself 0 points.

INTERVIEWER'S QUESTION

[9] "Give me an example of a time when you had to work on a team. What role did you play?"

Select the strongest answer.

[A] I've had good and bad experiences working with teams. One recent team project was in my marketing class. I was chosen to be the lead on a large project with 10 members of the class reporting to me. It was sort of an overwhelming number of people to deal with, but I guess that was part of the exercise. I hadn't really had much experience in managing people, but I learned fast—real fast. Some of the team members were motivated, and some were not. I found myself in several intense discussions trying to get those who were not motivated to be motivated. One thing I learned for sure is that I do not want to manage people in my career.

[B] One of my favorite activities as an MBA student is the group projects. In one of the projects I participated in, we had to put a marketing plan together. We decided we would all be equals, and so there was no leader. I did take it upon myself, however, to get contact information for each member. Since I was the strongest member in technology, it was a given that I would do the website and graphics. I had separate meetings with each team member to make sure I had everybody's input on the overall plan. I've never worked with a group that was so cohesive. Everything just fell into place. One of the members attributed a lot of the success of our project to my design work and the website I put together. I appreciated the acknowledgment—not to mention the A grade we received for the project.

[C] As a member of the intramural football team, I am in a team situation a great deal of the time. I am a person who likes to motivate people, and I am good at doing just that. I made it a point to talk to every member of my team and to find out a little about each person, trying to connect with each one in some way. I also made it a point to do a lot of "high fives" when someone played well. I was also very supportive when someone missed the ball, because I know how that feels. I was voted the player with the most team spirit in our end-of-season award dinner. That gesture made me feel like I had contributed to the spirit of the team, and that's even better than making a touchdown—almost.

ANSWERS

The Strongest Answer

[**B**] This is the strongest answer because it recounts a specific time when you made a difference in a team project—communicating and relating with others. Even though you were not the leader of this project, it was clear that you took the initiative to take a leadership role in organizing and planning. While you are answering one question, many other factors are being revealed from your story: initiative, strong technical knowledge, ability to explain technology, communication, and ability to work collaboratively by taking others' ideas into consideration. That's significant information to come out of one story.

The Mediocre Answer

[**C**] This is an OK answer. Your answer describes the situation: it tells what your role was—a team member; it relates how you motivated the team by interacting with the individual players; and it notes how you were rewarded by your behavior, both by receiving an honor and by feeling good about it. It would be a stronger answer if it were about one specific game or incident when you affected an individual's behavior.

The Weakest Answer

[**A**] The tone alone in this answer tells you this is a weak answer. It is negative from the beginning and goes downhill all the way. In this answer, you have ruled yourself out of any kind of position that requires leadership by stating that you don't want any part of it. That's OK if you have made a decision not to be a manager. However, short-term thinking can change, and it is best not to rule out all opportunities based on one bad experience.

RATE YOURSELF

If you chose answer [**B**], give yourself 5 points.

If you chose answer [**C**], give yourself 3 points.

If you chose answer [**A**], give yourself 0 points.

INTERVIEWER'S QUESTION

[10] "Pick one word to describe yourself. Why did you pick that word?"

Select the strongest answer.

[A] That would be *intense*. The reason I chose that word is because everything I do is important to me, and I always give it my all. If something gets in the way or challenges my results, I just keep pushing and working to get around it to meet my goal—whatever that is. I am that way both as a person and as a worker.

[B] I don't have one word that describes me. I am a lot of things in different situations. I guess if I had to choose one word it would be *flexible*. I adapt to change and can adjust quickly to new situations. I am known for being someone that can be called on at the last minute, and I will respond and get the job done if at all possible.

[C] *Hardworking*. I say that because I always do my best to work above and beyond expectations.

ANSWERS

The Strongest Answer

[**B**] This is the strongest answer because it takes advantage of the opportunity to tell the interviewer more than what was asked for but at the same time still answers the question. This answer deals with the question by answering with an explanation. That's a good technique to use to set up an answer that is not an exact match to the question asked; it's like putting a spin on the answer. By stating "I am known for being . . . ," you back up your claim with your reputation—and that's a positive. It would be an even stronger answer if you used a "third-party endorsement" by saying "My fellow students and bosses whom I have worked for have told me how much my being adaptable helps them."

The Mediocre Answer

[**A**] This is an OK answer. What saves this answer is that it doesn't use one word to answer the question. The answer explains why you chose that answer. If possible, it is a good rule not to answer a question with a single word. One of the objects of the interview is to let the interviewer get to know you, and if you only use one word to answer a question, you will miss out on an opportunity to tell more about yourself.

The Weakest Answer

[**C**] This answer is too vague and very trite. "Hard working" is probably the most overused trait used to answer questions about strengths and uniqueness. You did answer the question asked: "Why did you pick that word?" and that was a positive.

RATE YOURSELF

If you chose answer [**B**], give yourself 5 points.

If you chose answer [**A**], give yourself 3 points.

If you chose answer [**C**], give yourself 0 points.

Interview IQ Scorecard: What's Your Interview IQ Score?

Insert your score for each question in the blank following it. Then calculate your total score for the 10 questions.

Students and New Graduates Questions

1. "Did you have any problems getting here this morning?" _____

2. "Tell me about yourself." _____

3. "Why do you want to work for this company?" _____

4. "What do you think that you can bring to this position?" _____

5. "Tell me about a time when you had to deal with a difficult person." _____

6. "Tell me about the biggest project that you were involved in in school or in your personal life." _____

7. "Tell about a time when you had many projects with the same deadline and how you handled the situation." _____

8. "Do you have any questions?" _____

9. "Give me an example of a time when you had to work on a team. What role did you play?" _____

10. "Pick one word to describe yourself. Why did you pick that word?" _____

Index

About the Author

Carole Martin is an expert on interviewing and salary negotiation for the interviewer and the candidate. She is a speaker at conferences, business meetings, and classes. In addition to publishing many articles, she has authored six books on the subject of interviewing and hiring (five are published by McGraw-Hill): *Interview Fitness Training, Boost Your Interview IQ, Perfect Phrases for the Perfect Interview, Boost Your Hiring IQ, Perfect Phrases for Successful Job Seekers* (coauthor), and *Perfect Phrases for Writing Job Descriptions.*

Carole has more than 20 years of experience in human resources management in various industries including biotechnology, aerospace, software engineering, sales, publishing, and consulting. She is an acknowledged expert in the use of behavioral interviewing techniques and has made interviewing her specialty.

She has interviewed thousands of candidates at all levels in the corporate environment, as well as in academia and in nonprofit and government environments. Carole teaches her tips and techniques to job searchers and employers through one-on-one sessions, phone coaching, and group workshops. Thanks to the Internet, she has coached people across the United States and as far away as London, Paris, and Israel. She has a certification process to certify coaches in her methodology of interview coaching.

Carole holds a master's degree in career development from John F. Kennedy University in Pleasant Hill, California. In addition, she has been certified by the Human Resources Certification Institute as a Senior Professional in Human Resources.

As an adjunct faculty member at John F. Kennedy University, Carole has taught interviewing skills to counselors. She has also been an adjunct coach in the Haas Business School at the University of California, Berkeley, for six years and has worked with MBA students at Washington University in St. Louis.

You can access Carole's website at http://www.interviewcoach.com.